Treasures from the
Bunk Bed

(Naw, That's Not Grandma, That's Neena!)

Be joyful always. 1 Thess. 5:16

Linda Traugott

Linda Tracy Traugott

Edited by Sheri Mock

Photo Credit by: Mark Kidd Studios, Lexington,
Kentucky. markkiddstudios.com

ISBN 978-1-68517-406-4 (paperback)
ISBN 978-1-68517-407-1 (digital)

Christian Faith Publishing
832 Park Avenue
Meadville, PA 16335
www.christianfaithpublishing.com

Printed in the United States of America

Contents

Introduction

Children are a heritage from the Lord.

—Psalms 127:3

This one thing I know for certain. God is full of surprises. My husband and I had pretty much settled into our retirement years at seventy-three and sixty-three years of age. Well, we thought we had. With family in Oklahoma, Texas, Florida and South Carolina, our future plans included some travel. You know the saying about well-laid plans.

In 2003, God put His plan into action. Our son called one day and asked, "Mom, are you sitting down? You and Dad are going to be grandparents." So just after Christmas, a baby boy named Tyler Wallace made his entrance into our lives and rocked our world.

Since this little guy and his parents lived seventy-five miles east of us, we kept I-64 hot, visiting this precious little boy. God was not finished with His surprises.

Fifteen months later, SURPRISE! God provided another little bundle of baby boy, given the name Tate Griffin.

When Tyler was just a baby, he heard his daddy call me "Mom" and his mommy and my husband call me "Linda." He couldn't say "Linda," so it came out "Neena." Funny how grandchildren usually find their own terms of endearment for their grandparents.

Our hearts began to be pulled toward being closer to those boys, and we were spending so much time travelling back and forth between Louisville and Lexington, I could name every exit coming and going as well as tell you which ones had a McDonald's.

An earlier study of the book of Jonah revealed to me that sometimes God "interrupt" our lives to teach us something, or to use us in some way to bring a blessing to someone (or two) and/or to bless us. Two years later, Derby Day, May 2007, on the very first night we landed in Lexington with our loaded moving van, the boys begged to spend the night with "Neena and Pawpaw." The beds were hurriedly put together, and we sort of "camped out" among boxes and furniture. Mommy and Daddy seemed delighted that they could have a little time for themselves. Having two boys fifteen months apart was a lot like having twins.

I realize now what an absolute blessing it was that we were able to spend a great deal of time with our grandsons. Mommy and Daddy were both busy with businesses, so we got to experience lots of "boy joy," right from day one.

I think it's worth mentioning too that when we were raising our own children, there didn't seem to be time to stop and really enjoy them, so I feel that God gave us a second chance (or maybe a chance to do some things better). While writing this, my memory was jogged, and I did include a couple of things remembered about my own two children. I inserted these at the end of the book.

Our son-in-love custom-built bunk beds for our little ones, or T and T, as I affectionately refer to them sometimes. Since *Angry Birds* was the current fad, we decorated the beds with Angry Bird bedspreads, blankets, and stuffed Angry Birds.

Bedtime became my favorite time of the day, and I could hardly wait each night to hear what "jewel" might pop from one of their mouths, especially at prayer time. By morning, I would have forgotten the nugget I had heard, so I kept a pad and pen under the bed so I could jot a word to remind me later. They did not know I was keeping a diary. My entries are just as I wrote them down with maybe an incomplete sentence or two. Remember, kids say the darndest things, and these two proved it true time after time. Some of these stories are hilarious, but all exhibit the innocence and openness of a child.

One thing we tried to teach the boys was that if something was important to them, it was important to us. If they needed to ask questions or talk about something, nothing was off limits, as evidenced in these pages.

After sharing some of my *treasures* with friends and family, they encouraged me to write this book. I've come to understand a little more the story in Luke 2:19 of the birth of Jesus, when Mary, His mother, after the shepherds had visited, "treasured up all those things and pondered them in her heart." After pondering for a few years, I have begun this wonderful trip down memory lane.

There is a deep bond between a grandmother and her grandchildren. In my mind, I see a golden thread that stitches the fabric of our lives together, that sometimes takes an occasional detour through heartache, loss, and disappointment, but also fills out the tapestry with wonderful joy-filled experiences that bring a lifetime of precious memories.

And so I want to unpack my treasure trunk by sharing these golden nuggets of memory with you.

Treasures from the Bunk Bed

A Typical Day in This Grandma's Life

5:00 a.m.	Wake up, have coffee, pray
5:30 a.m.	Wake Gene up
5:45 a.m.	Check computer message
6:25 a.m.	Wake boys and take breakfast order
6:35 a.m.	Fix breakfast order
6:50 a.m.	Clothes laid out for boys
7:10 a.m.	Boys off to school
7:30 a.m.	Clean kitchen and make beds
8:00 a.m.	Breakfast for Gene and myself
8:30 a.m.	Take shower and makeup
9:00 a.m.	Sort and load washer
9:30 a.m.	Clothes to dryer
9:45 a.m.	Cut Pawpaw's hair
10:30 a.m.	Sort through paper and receipts
11:30 a.m.	Grocery for roast
Noon	Prepare roast for dinner
1:00 p.m.	Write checks, pay bills
2:30 p.m.	Pick up boys from school
3:30 p.m.	Conference with Tate's teacher
4:00 p.m.	Carrots in roast
4:10 p.m.	Fold clothes
5:00 p.m.	Potatoes in roast

Treasures from the Bunk Bed

5:30 p.m.	Open house at Southern Elementary
6:00 p.m.	Serve dinner
6:30 p.m.	Clean up dishes
7:45 p.m.	Start baths
8:15 p.m.	Ice cream for the boys
8:30 p.m.	In bed
9:00 p.m.	Prayers

Poem to Tyler and Tate

Surely you are angels sent here from above.
God made you very special, just for us to love.
You're like rays of sunshine, you precious little boys.
You just make our hearts sing, adorable bundles of joy.

With every day that passes, we can watch you grow.
We are just amazed that God has blessed us so.
Your little cherub faces, your tiny hands and feet.
God made you so perfect and did we mention sweet?

You are so amazing, we love everything about you.
Now we wonder how in the world we ever lived without you.
You brighten each and every day and light up all our nights.
With those million dollar smiles and your squeals of sheer delight.

The love we feel for both of you goes beyond all measure.
To us you two just hung the moon, you special little treasures.
The memories have just started, there'll be lots more too.
We'll ALWAYS love you, little guys, just because you're you.

         —Pawpaw and Neena

Acknowledgments

My daughter has helped with topics and scripture and many other areas I hadn't even thought of. She's actually the writer in the family. Our hope and purpose is that reading it will bring a smile to your day and, if it has been your good fortune to have spent time with grandchildren or other little ones that you love, it will prompt some sweet treasured memories of your own.

I tried to use each of these treasures for a teaching moment at the time, sometimes a social lesson, sometimes spiritual, or times of sharing, or just a time to love on two little boys who completely changed our life and filled it with more love than we could ever have imagined. Some were just so funny, they are little extra treasures.

Keep in mind that these little guys were three and four when I began to keep a diary of sorts. I became more serious about writing things down when they were about six and seven. The topics we discussed changed a lot by the time they were fifteen and sixteen.

I especially thank my dear friend Joy Wombles, who was my main encourager for this endeavor.

Curiosity

Sometime in 2008

Out of the clear blue sky, Tyler sweetly asked, "Neena, will you be my babies' mommy?" I said, "Well, sweetie, I'm too old to have babies." To which he replied, "But my babies are in your belly." Oh, the sweet innocence of a little child. Try to explain that one to a four-year-old.

After attempting several times to clear his throat, Tyler, four years old at the time, looked at me and said, "Neena, I have a frog in my mouth." He had heard us many times clearing the "frog" from our throat. We sometimes don't realize how much our children and grandchildren imitate us.

We were at elementary school for grandparents' night. Walking with PawPaw and me down the hall, one of Tate's teachers passed and asked Tate, "Oh, is this your grandma?" Tate replied, "Naw, that's not Grandma, that's Neena."

As the music played on TV, Tyler took my hand and said, "Will you dance with me, Neena?"

"Of course, I will dance with you, sweet boy. There is nothing I'd love more."

Tate was about three years old. We were putting together a wooden puzzle. When he could recognize what it was, he exclaimed, "Oh wookee, Neena, it's a widdle puppy!"

> In the beginning, things were in chaos and God
> brought it all together. (Genesis 1)

Chloe, our little friend whose grandmother lives next door, was standing in the driveway when five-year-old Tyler was leaving with his mom. Just before he got in the Denali, Tate turned the key in the ignition and rap music blared out. Tyler stepped back out of the Denali and, holding to the door, said, "Chloe, watch my moves," and proceeded to dance. It was darling. Very young children are so innocent and uninhibited.

No date

One of those "pop" questions.
TATE. Neena, do you have a butt?
ME. Well yes, Tate, I do. I think most everybody has one.
　　(Curiosity satisfied.)

September 23, 2012

Gathered fixin's for a sandwich, including a tomato I had taken a slice of on Thursday. Upon inspection, the tomato looked strange, shriveled, and dry. So that's what Tyler meant when he told me "Neena, I sucked all the juice outta your tomato."

September 30, 2012

Want a good laugh? Well I took off my jacket in the kitchen, which left me wearing black pants and a black tank top. Tyler came through the kitchen, looked at me, and said, "Hey, Neena, you look

HOT. I'm gonna keep him around. AND I'm gonna keep his glasses hidden right where they are.

Tate's prayer last night: "And, God, help Santa Claus to be safe when he travels all over the world and don't let anybody shoot him."

What a shame we live in such a violent time; our little ones have to worry about Santa getting shot.

TATE. Neena, is this my bad finger (as he held up his middle finger)?

I had some fast explaining to do.

ME. Well, your finger isn't bad, but that is a sign of something that doesn't have a nice meaning.

Constant teaching although he would not understand at this young age.

A couple of nights ago as I was lying in that place where I've learned so much, Tyler told me that Tate had kicked him "there" and his daddy got mad and told Tate he mustn't hit his brother there because "he might want to have children one day." I guess he pondered on that, and his question to me that night was, "Neena, how in the world can that make a baby?" I said, "Uh...uh...well... uh...[Lord, I could use a little help here]...uh!" Suddenly, he was fast asleep. Thank you, Lord, for rescuing me once again. Guess my 'splainin' days are not over just yet.

Lying on my back next to Tyler, he suddenly rolled over on top of me, his face looking right into mine. It startled me and I exclaimed, "WHAT ARE YOU DOING?" Sweetly he said, "Neena, I just wanna be your blanket."

Oh, the precious uninhibited love of a little child. (Well, maybe he's gonna be a country music songwriter, ha.)

I can remember grieving the time when my own children would lose that innocent view of their world. As it always happens, that time came and went. Now, I grieve for that of my grandsons. We can only do our best to supply them with tools for survival and pray that they use them. "Start children off on the way they should go, and even when they are old they will not turn from it" (Proverbs 22:6 NIV). I heard the testimony years ago of a mother whose children had become involved in the worlds of drugs as teens. She pointed out that in that scripture, it doesn't say that they will not be influenced by peers to ever stray, but the promise is that they will return to their spiritual roots. I can testify to that truth.

June 19, 2013

Home from VBS. Our youngest grandson told us last year that he was "going to trade my old dirty heart for a new clean one." He will be baptized soon. That makes both of them and that has been the desire of my heart for the last nine years—God is faithful. "Train up a child…" (Proverbs 22:6).

July 21, 2013

When our munchkins were telling us about their fun at Coney Island last Wednesday, Tate told us his tennis shoes and socks were all wet because he "fell in" the lake. We found out today from his chaperone that he didn't fall in at all—he just hauled off and jumped right in. BIG SURPRISE! That's why at that age, they have to have chaperones.

Last night in the twin bed, Tyler said, "I just don't get it, Neena. How can somebody pee on their self if they're asleep?"

Leave it to eight- and nine-year-old boys to teach Grandma that there is more than one definition to some words, like *package*. Hey, if you don't know what it is, I ain't gonna tell ya.

Gotta brag a little on my grandson. Driving to Toys "R" Us, we had to stop at the light at Circle 4 and Nicholasville Road, where an obviously homeless man stood with a sign that read "anything will help." Tate said, "Neena, can I give him my cold bottle of water. I haven't opened it." I said "Sure." He opened his window and asked the man if he'd like a cold bottle of water. The man said, "Yes, I would, thank you." (A great time to point to scripture. "Whatever you did for one of the least of these, you did for me" [Jesus, Matthew 25:40].) Sometimes these kids surprise us. Compassion for others is a God thing.

I showed T and T some bags of train sets from their "babyhood" and said, "Hey, guys, don't you think we should give these away to some little boys to play with?"

Tate looked at them and said wistfully, "Yeah…those were some good times!"

Lying down with Tyler one night recently, the night light was shining across my face.

TYLER. Neena, did you know you have a big nose?

ME. Well, you know I always had a pretty average-sized nose until I had you two grandsons, but I think God made my nose bigger so I can tell if you have brushed your teeth and washed under your arms.

October 15, 2013

When I picked up the boys at school yesterday, Tate piled in the front seat, Tyler in the back. We had barely pulled away from the school when Tyler asked, "Neena, why do you have your hair cut like a boy?"

November 26, 2013

My son finally gave his son a pocketknife while we were at Natural Bridge over the weekend. Monday morning, I said, "Please don't forget and take the knife to school." Uh-hummmmm! Well, after Gene left for school with the boys, I did not see the knife and almost had a heart attack. I knew that if a kid could get suspended for biting a Pop-Tart into the shape of a gun, then surely Tyler would be hauled off to juvie and become the target of an investigation on local TV, and we'd all end up in the pokey. Gene and I took this house apart, still did not find it. He drove back to school, and they called Tyler to the office with instructions to bring his jacket, lunch bag, and backpack. Gene said that the look on Tyler's face was indescribable. When he found out what he was called in for, he looked at Gene and said, "Pawpaw, I laid the knife on the back seat before I got out." And guess what, that's exactly where it was. We have put the knife up, and his touching it will be closely supervised.

December 18, 2013

Last night was a mixed bag around here. T and T were sitting on the sofa, one on my laptop, the other looking on, when I hear "Move over, you're right on top of me..." Then after a minute or two I hear,

"Stop breathing on me...move, you're breathing on me... Neena, MAKE HIM STOP BREATHING ON ME." Later, Tyler takes his tablet in the bathroom, and after I struggle with him to get it out of there, it plops right into the bathtub full of water. Oh...and then he refused to get in the bathtub because he said "There is probably electricity in that water." I had to let out the water and refill the tub. Didn't seem to hurt the tablet. It's working just fine today. "The steadfast love of the Lord never ceases. His mercies are new every morning. Great is your faithfulness" (Lamentations 3:22–23).

October 6, 2014

One thing is sure. My life is NOT boring. Picked up boys from school today.

TATE. Neena, guess what book is in the school library.
ME. Okay, what book is in the library?
HE. The name of the book is "———" (a part of the female anatomy.)
ME. How did you know about that book?
HE. A girl showed it to me.
ME. Did you look at it?
HE. No! (as he shook his head).

KIDS ARE SO MUCH FUN!

July 13, 2014

Lying between Tate and Tyler last night just after prayers, Tyler says, "I think I feel a hair growing on my leg, Neena. Can you feel it when a hair grows on your leg? Does it kinda sting?"

July 14, 2014

After praying for the future spouses of my grandsons last evening, these was a pause, then this comment:

TATE. Neena, when a guy and girl get married, does a baby get started on the wedding night?

ME. (After a big gulp) Well, sometimes it does happen that way, Tate.

Last night, after Tate said his prayers, Tyler whispered in my ear, "When are you going to tell him the truth?"

"About what?"

"That there really is no tooth fairy, or Santa Claus, or Easter Bunny. When you gonna tell him?"

TATE. Tell me what?

TYLER. That the tooth fairy, Santa Claus, and Easter Bunny are not real.

TATE. Oh yes, they are, 'cause Dad told me.

TYLER. Yeah, then where does the tooth fairy live, huh? Tell me that.

TATE. Dad said she lives in a big tree and keeps all the teeth there.

TYLER. Neena, please tell him they're all fake? His friends will make fun of him.

TATE. Don't tell me anything.

(Sometimes we just don't want to hear the truth. It may shake our world.)

Trying to get past a fall head cold (sore throat, voice loss), which I seem to get every year about the time I get out the Christmas tree and deco…hmmmmm. Had promised the boys I'd take them shopping to buy gifts for those on their lists. Their personalities always take over. Between them, Tyler is the one who enjoys spending all his money and then some, but his generous and loving spirit is so sweet.

Tate, on the other hand, will wind up with "money in the bank" and have fun watching others spend theirs. Haha!

TATE. Neena, I guess you have another shirt under the one that's under your vest?

ME. Yes, I do.

TATE. And you have a bra on under that?

ME. Yes, I do.

TATE. Well I guess you could call your bra a "breast warmer."

ME. I guess you could, Tate.

Haha! Boys!

Grandsons (fourth and fifth grade) are learning things fast—things I didn't hear about until at least junior high. So on the way home from school with Tyler (Tate at school auditioning for a part in Cinderella), he asks about something a cousin told him about human anatomy. In trying to explain it, my eye was drawn to the car's ignition. So... I explained that a lot of things are referred to as male and female; in this case the ignition being female and the key being male, a reference to wall plugs, etc. When we picked Tate up, Ty tells him all about what he had learned. I wake up every morning asking, "Okay, God, what is the challenge today?" Never a dull moment at our house. "Male and female He created them" (Genesis 5:2).

TYLER. Neena, they are going to show a video at school about puberty.

TATE. Do the boys and girls have to watch it together?

TYLER. Naw, the boys have one video and the girls have two.

ME. Wonder why the girls have two?

TATE. Probably 'cause girls have more stuff.

"Male and female He created them" (Genesis 5:2).

March 25, 2015

Tyler, *as he walks in from school with a cat-ate-the-mouse grin.* Neena, we saw the "puberty" video today.

Me. Did you learn anything new?

Tyler. Yes, but we're not supposed to talk about it to kindergartners because they'll start laughing. They're just too immature. It's only for fifth graders on up to know about that.

Me. I'd say that's probably true.

Tyler. Yeah, I walked in the room a kid and came out a man.

Me, *to myself.* Teehee.

April 26, 2015

Thought I'd turn in early and relax listening to the radio. The boys have knotted up every pair of earbuds in this house. I finally found a pair. Ever try to untangle earbuds in the dark? What a mess. Had to get up, go to the kitchen in a good light with my readers on. So now I'm so keyed up I could jump in the ring with Muhammad Ali. So much for relaxing.

July 20, 2015

Tyler. It's gonna feel really weird going to middle school this year 'cause some of those guys even have mustaches.

August 20, 2015

After killing a quarter-sized black spider in the bathroom, I had to lie down with our boys. Tyler asked me to "bear-hug" him. In a few minutes, I asked, "Aren't you getting warm?" He replied, "Yes, but that's good... I feel like a roasted marshmallow." I told him that's how I feel when scary things crawl into my life. God wraps himself around me and I feel like a roasted marshmallow.

December 3, 2015

Tate refuses to admit there is no Santa. It's driving Tyler crazy.

December 3, 2015

Had to run into Walmart, Tyler with me. He said, "I need some more cologne. Mine is almost gone."

"Okay, I'm gonna pick up bread, and you pick out your cologne." He obviously had sprayed some on because I almost choked in the car. When I asked what kind it was, he said, "New York Playboy... Neena? What's a playboy?"

I told him it was a guy who likes girls.

He said, "Well, that'll work...'cause I like girls."

July 29, 2016

So I stopped at the fruit market to get fresh tomatoes for my BLT and got three beautiful peaches. I walk into the kitchen last night to catch Tyler juggling the peaches. First bite this morning is a bruise. Grrrrr!

September 13, 2016

Ahhhhh...the sweet aroma that emanates upon opening the bedroom door at 7:00 a.m. where two middle-school-age boys have been sleeping, snoring, and breathing all night.

December 2, 2016

Tyler was sitting beside me in church Sunday morning. He put his head over on me and smiled sweetly. He turned to our friend on

Treasures from the Bunk Bed

the other side and whispered in her ear. I found out later that he told her "old people are soft."

December 17, 2017

Sitting beside Tyler this morning (in church) and after he had his head on my shoulder, he writes on the bulletin, "Why is your ear so soft?"

Write down your favorite memories with your
grandchildren on these journal pages

_____
_____
_____
_____
_____
_____
_____
_____
_____
_____
_____
_____
_____
_____
_____
_____
_____
_____
_____
_____
_____
_____
_____
_____
_____
_____
_____
_____
_____
_____
_____
_____
_____
_____

Write down your favorite memories with your
grandchildren on these journal pages

_____
_____
_____
_____
_____
_____
_____
_____
_____
_____
_____
_____
_____
_____
_____
_____
_____
_____
_____
_____
_____
_____
_____
_____
_____
_____
_____
_____
_____
_____
_____
_____
_____

Love and Assurance

Love is patient, love is kind. It does not envy, it does not boast,
it is not proud. It does not dishonor others, it is not self-seeking,
it is not easily angered, it keeps no record of wrongs.
—1 Corinthians 13:4–5 (NIV)

Every child deserves to know he/she is loved.

Preschool 2009

When one of Tate's teachers asked him about a sore he had on his leg, he replied, "I hurt it and Daddy put 'roxide on it." Such cuteness!

April 25, 2010

Great weekend. Fun with the boys here overnight. Love sleeping beside those little guys. The day will come too soon when they would rather eat brussels sprouts than sleep with Neena, so I treasure every minute I get to cuddle with them. We went to Sunday school, church, then enjoyed a good day with Daddy also. Now I'm exhausted.

January 25, 2011

So with grandsons seven and five, pulling up to Subway Sunday for lunch after church to meet Erik and Gene...five-year old says, "Wow, Pawpaw looks nice in his clothes."

May 1, 2012

Gene and I surprised our grandsons today and had a taco lunch at school.

No date—Random thought

Sweethearts! I love them. They're two of the main reasons I get out of bed every morning.

August 2, 2012

Riding to GattiTown with Tyler. Talking about Uncle Otto building their bunk beds. I said, "Just think, Tyler, one day you will want one of the beds and Tate will want one, your sons will sleep in them, then your grandson will sleep in the bed your Uncle Otto made for you." He said, "Yeah, it'll be a family tradition." Tyler has always been all about family. I believe having family relationships are very important and can lend a source of security. Unconditional family love demonstrates God's love for us. ("But God demonstrates his own love for us in that while we were still sinners Christ died for us" [Romans 5:8].)

Okay, on the way to the park to go fishing with our son and his boys, eight-year-old looks at his daddy and says, "After we go fishing and catch some fish, can we make french fries and hush puppies?" PRICELESS!

Otto and Sheri came today bearing the bunk beds Otto built for our grandsons. What a beautiful labor of love. The boys are going to love them when they get back on Sunday. Super fantastic job, Otto. You are such a keeper (not to mention a true blessing in our lives).

September 17, 2012

It was an emotionally exhausting day. It's raining outside my window and inside my heart. I only wish I could absorb everyone's grief onto myself. Sleep well, loved ones, "JOY COMES IN THE MORNING." I know for I have been there many times in my life.

("Their sorrow was turned into joy [Esther 9:22].)

October 11, 2012

TYLER, *beside me in bed*. Neena, please wrap your arms around me and hug me really tight all night, or till I tell you to stop.

ME. Oh, Tyler, the arms of my heart will ALWAYS be wrapped tight around you, and this memory will be one of the treasures that are hidden deep in my heart. It was utter joy to give security to one of my grandchildren. ("He shall cover you with his feathers and under His wings you will be safe" [Psalms 91:4].)

November 11, 2012

As I was supervising the toothbrushing last night, grandson comes with paper in hand and asks, "Neena, how do you spell *sturb?*"

"Well, I don't believe I've ever heard that word. Use it in a sentence for me." He said, "Like DO NOT STERB" (another golden nugget in my treasure box of memories). He was writing a sign to go on their bedroom door. Private space is important for a child, a place where he can put his "important" things and a place where he feels safe and secure and maybe even think about things important to him.

January 29, 2013

Some kids will say or do anything to stay in bed a little longer in the morning. Tyler is just the opposite. I have always patted him on the back, rubbed his head, whatever it took to get him to sleep at night. Maybe that's why at 5:45 a.m., I heard "Neena," and when I went to check on him, he said, "What are you doing?" I said, "Sitting on the sofa, drinking coffee. Did you need something?" He said, "I want to come out there and cuddle with your hand. It smells good." Well…must be that A&D ointment on the cracked fingers. It made me think of the comfort I experience when God's awesome hand "rubs my head" when I have those moments of fear.

February 27, 2013

Lying down with the boys, Tate said he was scared (trying to manipulate me, of course). I said, "Why are you scared?" He said, "I got scared in the bathroom at church tonight. I didn't think anybody was in there, but I heard the trash can move." Tyler, wearing a smirk, said, "Well, Tate, maybe somebody was *in* the trash can."

March 30, 3013

I am one proud grandmother. Great report cards are a given for youngest, so not surprised with his "above levels" on nearly everything. The oldest brought home seven As and two Bs *plus* an honor roll certificate.

I thank God for an Awana teacher at church who offered tutoring because of her love for this precious little boy. What a blessing to Tyler. Some kids are very intelligent but just need that extra ounce of personal attention. Thank you, Lord, once again for answered prayer. Thanks to Mrs. Darlene. Thank you, Tyler, for all your hard work.

No Date

One night this week (from the top bunk).

TATE. Neena, I'm scared.
ME. What is scaring you?
TATE. The hamster.
ME. Why?

TATE. 'Cause he's starin' at me.

This became a lesson about fear and trusting God.

"The Lord is on my side; I will not fear" (Psalms 118:6). I told them about a young boy named David and how he killed a giant with a slingshot and a smooth stone. The giant was going to kill David's people. God will help you to overcome things that seem scary sometimes.

May 4, 2013

This week Gene told me that they were going to play Elvis movies during this month. Later, Tyler asked me about Elvis, and I said "Oh my gosh, I was so in love with Elvis. I had all his records." He said, "Were you going to marry him?"

I said, "Well, if he'd asked me, I probably would have."

Thursday night, Tyler told Gene, "Pawpaw, Neena wanted to marry Elvis, but he married somebody else. So that's why she married you." When I first saw Gene, he looked so much like Elvis. I fell in love quickly. We were married fifty-six years before he moved to his heavenly home where he waits for me.

May 4, 2013

Fifty-three minutes ago. You know you are getting old when your grandchildren pray that you "will wake up in the morning and not die during the night." It's quite reassuring. Haha!

June 25, 2013

Since the boys aren't here to say, "Yuk, what is that smell?" I thought it would be a good time to make a pot of bean soup (enough to freeze). I'm having flashbacks of Mom's Monday washday and the bean soup with pork jowl and onion smell permeating our little house. Tomorrow, I'll be cooking cabbage and potatoes. The boys *hate* that aroma more than the beans. Mmmmmm...good! (I hated all that when I was a kid also.)

September 29, 2013

I have experienced many things in my seventy years, but none has ever given me more pleasure than lying next to a child whose stomach is hurting, holding him close to warm his tummy, and praying for his comfort and healing as he drifts off to dream of puppy dogs and ice cream with the sweetest smile on his beautiful face. Being a grandmother has some of the greatest rewards in this world.

January 4, 2014

Just sitting here watching *Gaither Homecoming*, Jason Crabb singing "Thank You Lord for Your Blessings on Me." We don't think they're listening because they are playing on their tablets, earphones on, and not exactly music they would choose to listen to, but every now and then I hear Tyler humming along to "Thank You Lord for Saving my Soul." I treasure these sweet moments and pray these times will be hidden in their hearts and become treasures later in their lives. Uh-oh, Tyler just pulled a tooth, so I gotta run.

January 13, 2014

One sick eight-year-old boy, cup of tea, chicken noodle soup, Jell-O, pillow, blanket = busy and sympathetic Nurse Neena (I'd rather be sick myself).

January 14, 2014

Tate was not well today. After showers and a little chicken noodle soup, I gave them both a little ice cream (yes, I spoil them). When he finished, he put his hands on his forehead and announced, "I'm NORMAL. Neena, I'm NORMAL now." I'd say we'll have two at home from school tomorrow.

Treasures from the Bunk Bed

Tyler home today with a 102 temperature. I took them to their doc to rule out strep. Last night Tyler said, "Neena, if I have to stay home tomorrow, will you do all the things for me that you did for Tate?" (He overheard Tate tell the doctor that I had spoiled him.) Tate went to school but came home coughing worse than ever and completely wiped out. I have been giving them ibuprofen and Delsym. After sitting in a tub of tepid water to get his temp down from 103, Tyler decided to eat some chicken noodle soup. When he finished, he put his hands on his forehead and announced. "I'm NORMAL, Neena, I'm normal now."

I was up several times during the night peeping through the blinds, trying to figure out how bad the weather was going to be. On a school morning, Tyler has to be awakened slowly and pulled from the bed while I sing "Good Morning to You, We Live in a Zoo." But this morning, he was anticipating yet another snow day and, as I enjoyed my quiet time, came bouncing out of the bed at 5:07 a.m. Funny how that happens, huh? The cheerfulness soon disappeared when I told him the good news, "SCHOOL DAY." Hah!

TYLER. Neena, when you die, God gives you a new body, right?
ME. Yes, that's what the Bible says.
TYLER. Then why can't He give you a new body before you die so you can stay here with me?

Almost without fail, in the wee hours of the morning, I wake to find a thin little boy-body next to me. Last night, I felt someone climb over me and just assumed it was him. Around 4:00 a.m., I awoke to find Tyler standing beside my bed, and using his bossy voice, he said, "How did *he* get in here?" I realized that the boy in the bed beside me was Tate. I said, "Well, I guess he got in here the same way you usually do. He got out of the bed, walked in here, and piled in." (I had to get in Tyler's bed with him so he'd go back to sleep. I am BL.E.S.S.E.D. And always a little sleep-deprived.)

March 19, 2014

Tate's home from surgery and just soaking up all the attention. Tyler was the loving, caring big brother who made Tate laugh, which made Tate cry because it hurt so much. He was just trying to cheer him up. Well, sometimes humor can be painful, I guess.

March 28, 2014

This morning I had the highest compliment I could ever hope for from a child. And it leaves me with extreme accountability. I don't even remember what prompted it, but Tyler said, "Neena, I can trust you." Wow! That was really BIG!

August 8, 2014

We shopped yesterday and the day before for new shoes and clothes for school. On the way home, Tate said, "I don't think I'd want to be really, really rich." Tyler said, "Tate, I am rich—in God's love." He can be so sweet and two minutes later does something that makes you want to swat him. Gotta love 'em.

August 9, 2014

Rough night. Heavy heart. Too much sadness in our lives and world, but I am reminded that God knows our names. He sees our tears and listens when we pray. Yes, I woke with some songs in my heart. Our hope is in the Lord—hallelujah.

After a long, busy day, lying next to Tyler because he begged me to, he scoots real close and says, "I like sleeping with you because I feel safe…and you're so warm." When I go to bed at night, I can go to sleep confident that "the one [God] who watches over me will not be slumbering or sleeping" (Psalm 121:3–4).

Holding our puppy last night before bed, Tyler told her, "I love you so much, I would die for you." She loves him also, but she didn't say if she'd die for him…exactly. No one would die for us, but John 3:16 says that "God so loved the world that He gave his only son and whoever believes on Him will not perish but will live forever with Him."

TYLER. Neena, come back here with me.
TATE. You don't have to be afraid 'cause Pawpaw's back there.
TYLER. Yeah, that's what I'm afraid of.

Out the door after another stressful morning.

TATE. Neena, why aren't you dead?
ME. Gosh, why do you ask that?
TATE. Putting up with us, that's why.
ME. God may lose patience with me sometimes, but He never
    stops loving me.

(BTW, Tyler lost his electronics privileges for three days after his shenanigans this morning.)

A young couple sat across from us in church this morning. Daddy was holding his baby girl like a delicate flower, her head in his hand, and throughout the entire service, he examined her precious face as she adored him. He traced her tiny nose with his finger. He could not look away from her. She discovered her little fist and caught sight of it as she moved her arms. I couldn't help but offer a prayer for that sweet family. What a blessed little angel. Every child deserves to be loved like that. That is exactly how God loves me (and you).

After killing a quarter-sized black spider in the bathroom, I had to lie down with our boys. Tyler asked me to "bear-hug" him. In a few minutes, I asked, "Aren't you getting warm?" He replied, "Yes, but that's good… I feel like a roasted marshmallow." I told him that's how I feel when scary things crawl into my life. God wraps himself around me and I feel like a roasted marshmallow.

I love to sit and meditate and pray and plan my day, with my coffee in our darkened family room from 5:00 to 6:00 a.m., before the boys wake up and the tornado begins. Last night, Tyler asked me to get him up at 5:00. Tate said, "No, Tyler. That's Neena time." Thanks, Tate. Lord, I seek a quiet and humble spirit. "Search me, O God, and know my heart; try me, and know my thoughts" (Psalms 139:23 KJV).

I love to hear the boys whistle. It tells me that at that moment in time, they are feeling happy. Jiminy Cricket sang "Give a Little Whistle" in *Pinocchio*. (Dear Heavenly Father, may these two treasures that you have entrusted to my care always feel secure and happy in our home. Thank you, Lord, for the peace and security I find in you.)

In the door from school yesterday, Tate announced he was making dinner. He decided on breakfast for dinner. He fixed bacon, scrambled eggs, and toast with jelly. (Great job, Tate.) I think I could get used to this.

CONTENTMENT—the realization that God has used every experience in your life, good and bad, to equip you for this moment in time. God wastes nothing.

My memory just took me back to a holiday that I did not have to work. I was planning a shopping day. Just as I was headed out the door, the school called and informed me that my son, Erik, was in the office, sick. I picked him up, and by the time we reached the car, he was not sick anymore. When I asked, "You sure don't act sick. Why did you have them call me?" He replied, "Every kid needs a day with his mom, doesn't he?" Grrr, in hindsight, I should have marched him right back in the school. ("The Lord hates a lying tongue" [Proverbs 6:17].)

Erik, Tyler, and Tate could not wait to give me my Mother's Day gift. Then they told me they wanted a dessert made with it every week. Today's goody is lemon cake with lemon buttercream frosting. I love the KitchenAid.

NEENA. Momma said I should've been a preacher because I loved lengthy spiritual discussions with Daddy. Daddy said I should've been a lawyer because our discussions sometimes turned into a debate.

Grandsons said I should've been a talk show host because I had something to say about everything. Gene ain't sayin'.

Write down your favorite memories with your
grandchildren on these journal pages

_____
_____
_____
_____
_____
_____
_____
_____
_____
_____
_____
_____
_____
_____
_____
_____
_____
_____
_____
_____
_____
_____
_____
_____
_____
_____
_____
_____
_____
_____
_____
_____

Write down your favorite memories with your grandchildren on these journal pages

Nature/Creation

AGE is a quality of mind
If you have left your dreams behind
If hope is cold.
If you no longer look ahead
If your ambitions' fires are dead
Then you are old.

But if from life you take the best
And if in life you keep the jest
If love you hold.
No matter how the years go by
No matter how the birthdays fly
You are not old.

—Author Unknown

Tyler and I sat on the patio one warm afternoon. Tyler said, "Neena, you have cracks in your legs. Oh, look. My legs are so dry." It's amazing how early we begin to notice things like that. (Actually, the cracks are spider veins.)

No Date

TATE. Neena, why do you have your tomatoes lined up on the sink like bowling balls?

TATE. Neena, you have cracks in your neck.

ME. Yes, Tate, when you get older, you get cracks in lots of places. It's just part of the getting old thing.

No Date

If anyone had ever told me I'd be potty-training a hamster, I'd say, "You're crazy." I think I may need to get a life.

No Date

You know you are getting old when—your grandchildren pray that you "will wake up in the morning and not die during the night."

December 9, 2009

Taking the Santa train on the Bluegrass railway at the Bluegrass Railroad Museum at two o'clock with Daddy, Mommy, Tyler, and Tate. Don't you know they are excited? Santa and Mrs. Santa will be arriving on a firetruck and riding the train with us and spending time with each child. Now doesn't that sound like fun? This kid is gonna have a good time too. Do we ever grow up?

Took boys to professional photographer to have photos done. We left, and while driving home, I said, "Well, Tate, what did you think about Sassy the lamb?" Tate answered, "Was it real?" I said, "Well, the lady was wiping something up off the floor." Tate thought a minute and said, "Ohhhh…yeah!"

March 5, 2011

Our Taterbug is here for the night. We bought a Lego Missile Battery. Too difficult for my brain. Taking back tomorrow. We cannot figure it out, and believe me, he is way smarter than me.

October 23, 2011

Our two guys sang with the music makers at church this morning ("Gone Fishin'"). Tyler had his debut on the stage with a one-liner, and he did it beautifully with his fishin' pole, ball-hat turned sideways, and red bandana hangin' out his pocket. "Neena's delight." Getting ready to take them to choir practice right now

Tyler built a stage set for his puppets while here overnight. He loves all the artsy stuff, creating, building, and performing. Of course, I don't encourage it at all, haha! The kids are also getting ready for a musical drama at church.

Tuesday I picked up the grandsons from the school bus. Tyler handed me his backpack and it was so heavy I almost fell sideways. I asked what in the world was in there. Well, he had books from the library and right on top was his new Bible in the camouflage book carrier Uncle Otto and Aunt Sheri gave him when he was baptized Sunday. Erik took him to Kroger's Sunday night, and Tyler told total strangers, "I got baptized today." Go, Tyler! God, give me this kind of boldness!

My imagination went wild yesterday while I waited in the car for my son as I looked upon a very old large white frame farmhouse whose rooms went deep into the back of the house with a screened porch along the side. I could smell a sweet aroma of honeysuckle vines all along the fence row. I pulled a picture out of my memory of creaking wood floors and could almost hear the chatter at family meals and birthday parties. If those walls could talk, they'd tell of births and deaths, love won and lost, lively Rook games, a lot of joy and not a few tears. When my friend and I visit the nursing home Thursday, I'll see each resident like the old house. Behind the windows of their dimmed eyes and the frail walls of their aging bodies, lie memories which have become, though a little faded, golden nuggets of treasure…and we'll sing "Precious Memories, How They Linger."

I can hardly wait to lie down with the boys at night. They say the cutest things. Tonight, we were talking about the beginning of the world and creation of animals when Tyler said, "Neena, how did lions get so mean?" I said, "Well, I don't think God made them that way." He thought a moment then said, "Oh, I know what happened. People started pulling their tails, and it made 'em mad so they got mean." (Well, why not?)

My mom never worried about me walking the several blocks to the library in the 1940s. We thought terrible things only happened in Chicago, Cincinnati, or New York. I loved the library, where every Saturday, I would go to watch puppet shows like "Punch and Judy." Oh, how I loved books, and I checked out the limit every time. I would read them very quickly and head back for more. I learned early that reading allowed me to discover people and places all over the world that I'd probably never see or know. My grandsons always invite me to the school bookfair, knowing I'll buy some books for them. I have done my best to instill the pleasure of reading on to my children and grandchildren.

There is a hawk who is terrifying all the birds in our backyard. We have all seen him. He lives high in a tree in the yard of the sixteen thousand square foot house that overshadows our humble little home. The other day, I thought a man was looking over the fence at me; his face was so huge. Gene saw him down in the birdbath today taking a bath, splashing all the water out of the bowl. Somebody needs to STUFF THAT BIRD!

Yesterday was a perfect day to take a group of around twenty-five first through fourth graders to Fort Boonesborough. I was "bus mom" for twelve boys. Coming home, we all stopped at McDonald's for ice cream. At one table, the seven girls were typical chatty little girls. Three tables of boys were arm wrestling, poking holes in the sides of their cones, and sucking the ice cream out through the hole, and having a contest to see who could finish first. If you don't believe God created us *male* and *female* with distinct differences, come along on our next day trip.

Jacobson Park lake, pedal boats, sore leg muscles—that is all.

I was encouraged this week that maybe the creativity of our children is NOT completely down the tubes because of iPods and computer games. The boys played pool at the clubhouse at our son's apartment. They came back with their little wheels turning in their heads. They had already decided to turn my kitchen island on wheels into a pool table. They made balls out of colored construction paper and tape (even a white one), cue sticks out of rolled paper, pockets out of Styrofoam cups taped on the appropriate places. They played for a long time, and it was great. Kids need to use their creative gifts.

I'm looking forward to our little guys coming back tomorrow. I've missed them so much this week. As the old saying goes, "I wouldn't want them any other way." Things'll sure heat up around here though. One of them will say, "Neena, are you old?"

And I'll say, "Yes, but there are a few people older than me."

He'll say, "Hmm."

July 18, 2012

One of the most exciting things to do when I was a kid was to run around in the rain barefoot, walk in the gutters that were over-flowing, lie down and roll around in the low spots in the yard, and get soaking wet. Guess with all the sewer runoff, pesticides, etc., it wouldn't be a good idea to do that today. When it stormed, my dad would always sit on the front porch while thunder rolled and light-ning flashed all around. These days we like to sit in the garage with the door up and watch the show. We're teaching our grandsons to enjoy this simple pleasure. We had a really good one tonight while we were in church.

August 15, 2012

It is now about 9:40 a.m. on the first day of school. The boys were excited about it and had a hard time going to sleep. Then about 5:00 a.m., Tyler came and got in bed beside me and began to chatter, so about 5:45 I got up and turned on the coffee and the fish tank. So that's when that snail cleans the tank. I've never seen him move so fast. And Frog was having a ball jumping as though he was on a trampoline. I just now got this house back in some kind of order (but the first day was a lot of fun), and I'm heading back for a nap.

Driving home from school, I pull next to an SUV with the cutest dog hanging halfway out the window. When Tate sees him, he says, "Neena, I read his lips, and he's singing. 'When I walk in the spot (yeah), this is what I see (okay)…everybody stops and they staring at me… I'm sexy and I know it.'" These guys are giving me an education. First time I ever heard a dog rappin'.

October 6, 2012

If I had a decent camera, I'd take a picture of our newest family member, a cute furry hamster the boys named "Fuz." He ran a round trip to Dallas on his wheel last night. He (or she? I forgot to ask at the pet store) is a little cutie. I heard Tyler say, "I love you, Fuz. I love you soooooo much." Pets teach children about love, responsibility, and much more.

In an effort to delay getting clothes on for school, nine-year-old reads Isaiah 55:12 and exclaims, "Neena, what does it mean 'the mountains and hills will burst into song, and the trees of the field with clap their hands?'"

I said, "Well, I think it means that if *we* don't praise God, the rocks and hills and all God's other creations will praise Him in our place."

He replied, "Ewwwwww, I DO NOT want Bob the Builder land, where everything, even the tractors, talk."

March 3, 2013

Somehow reptiles were a topic of conversation in bed tonight.

ME. What are amphibians?
TYLER. Well, they're part lizard and part worm. But the big ones are a-stink. Like dinosaurs, Neena, they're a-stink too.
ME. Yeah, I'll bet.

March 26, 2013

When I lay my tired body down last night, I really thought I'd not be able to get out of bed, and Gene would have to take me to Urgent treatment center to yank out all the kinks I tied myself into last night. While Tate was taking a shower, I wrestled on the floor with Tyler. After Tate's shower, he begged me, "Neena, wrestle me like you did Tyler." I had to, of course. Oh my gosh! Seventy-three-year-old grandmas have no business wrestling.

April 11, 2013

On the way to the dentist for cleaning:

TATE. Neena, does a snake have a butt?

Me. Well, I don't know, but I think it would be hard to find.
Tyler. Well, I'm not gonna lift his tail and look.

He drew this picture waiting to leave for school this morning…ha!

June 2, 2013

Before sleep last night, we were discussing getting old (i.e., how old I'd be in twenty years). Tyler said, "Will you live to be one hundred?" Tate says, "Well, if she lives in Winchester and she lives to be one hundred, her picture will be on a soup can."

April 23, 2013

Both boys have stuffed snakes about five feet long that lay in their bunks. Last night, Tate let his hang down just far enough that

Tyler grabbed it and pulled so hard, the tongue came out of its mouth and landed on the floor. Tyler said, "Oh, that's all right. Neena can sew it back on. She sewed my snake back together one time." I said I would do that today. After a moment or two, I heard Tate say, "Don't sew it, Neena, he doesn't even need a tongue."

July 3, 2013

A couple of years ago, Tyler and I went to the Creation Museum in Newport, Kentucky. He bought a tiny toy alligator, which we put in water and watched it "grow" over a few days. It shrinks back down a little when not in water. It has been back in water in a heart-shaped bowl in the kitchen for about a week or so. Last night, I happened to look around and caught Tyler turning up that bowl with the alligator and taking a big drink. Oh, yuk. (Boys! They are a "special" breed!)

July 14, 2013

Riding the church bus next to first grader last Wednesday on the way to Monkey Joe's for 'wonderful Wednesday' outing. With the sun shining in on us, he talked my leg off and suddenly looking at me said, "You have a lot of wrinkles in your face." I said, "Yes, I do, and you know what? It cost more to get them than it would cost to get rid of them." There is no way he could understand. Some things that life hands you (by choice or by chance) carry a price tag of pain and sleepless nights. And though God faithfully sees us through, we sometimes wind up wearing the results.

August 9, 2013

Getting ready to take boys for before-school physicals, I put on a black tank to wear a shirt over and walk through the family room. Tate gasps. "Why would *you* want to wear a top like that?" I guess it's good that they are so observant. I ought to get in the car like this and watch him really freak out. Hehe!

"Neena, do you have any more of those…uh…things…they look like a…an apricot…you know with a line down the middle and little lines going out from that, and I really like 'em? You had some in a Ziploc bag?" After a few guesses (i.e., grapes, raisins, limes?), a light came on, and I said, "Pecans?" He said, "*Yeah*, that's what they are. I'm just dying for some of those!"

When Tyler brought his cello home, he told me his homework was to "practice until you drive everybody in the house crazy." Well, he hasn't practiced hardly at all, *but* I can now play the D and E without even looking and intend to be able to play this booger by the end of the semester. Maybe I'll just sit in for him for the Christmas concert. Teehee!

Lying with my little cello player last night, I asked if he is learning anything, he said, yes. Then he began singing D-D-D-D, E-E-E-E, F#, E-E, D. Then fell asleep.

Right in the middle of Tyler's prayer last night, "Neena, how old will I be when you're one hundred?"

"Oh, you'll be thirty-seven."

"God, make Neena live till she's a hundred and twenty-three."

Tate leans over the top bunk and says, "Tyler, that's too old. She won't be able to take care of herself."

("Very truly I tell you, when you were younger you dressed yourself and went where you wanted; but when you are old you will stretch out your hands, and someone else will dress you and lead you where you do not want to go" [John 21:18 NIV].)

When the garage door goes down, and they are on their way to school, would it be a sacrilege to break into a rousing chorus of "HALLELUJAH, HALLELUJAH" from Handel's "Messiah"?

It seems like these boys need new tennis shoes every couple of months; they grow so fast. So we paid a visit to Shoe Carnival. Tyler couldn't find any shoes to suit him in the kid's shoes, so I suggested we go to the men's shoes while Erik helped Tate.

> TYLER. Neena, I think this is a new page in my life, don't you?
> ME. A new page. How?
> TYLER. I'm getting shoes in a man's size. (Well, he found some blue ones, and I thought they looked too wide, but try arguing with a ten-year-old when he says they feel great and he loves them.)

So we went back for Dad's approval.

> ERIK. Tyler, you look ridiculous. They're way too big, and you look like a duck. Put 'em back. I'm not buying shoes too big. (Dad won that one, of course.)

Guess that "new page" will remain blank for a while. (We did find shoes in kid's department.)

We had a conversation about the spider veins behind my knees earlier in the evening. As I was washing my face last night, Tate walked in.

ME. I wish I could just wipe off my old face and wipe on my thirty-five-year-old face.
TATE. That would *not* be good.
ME. Why not?
TATE. 'Cause then your face would *not* match your legs.

March 30, 2014

When the boys and I were discussing getting a dog a couple of weeks ago, Tyler thought about it and said, "Neena, we should go to the humane society and get an "ugly" dog that nobody else wants." He can be as much a stinker as any other ten-year-old, but that tells me a lot about his heart. I feel kind of guilty that I wound up getting such a cutie dog. But I found her through a good friend. Maybe we can still get an "ugly" dog.

May 19, 2014

Nine-year-old comes in from school today, says, "I'm not gonna get on my tablet today. I'm gonna play basketball, ride my bike, kick the soccer ball around, hit some tennis balls. What else can I do to lose weight and get stronger?"

I say, "Well, I guess you could work out by doing sit-ups and push-ups."

He says, "Well, I'd like to eat some carrots and apples too."

I say, "Gosh, I'm really proud that you want to improve that way. That's great."

He says, "I wouldn't be doing all this, but I have a new girlfriend. She's really hot, and I want to get fit."

Gosh! They start early these days.

August 11, 2014

Sometimes, right in the middle of a personal crisis, a child can make you laugh your socks off. Yesterday, our choir sang, "We'll Soon Be Done," and there is a line that says "Soon I will be done with the troubles of this world, troubles of this world, troubles of this world…" I was cleaning up the dishes this morning and singing this line when Tyler asked, "Are you saying troubles of the squirrel, troubles of the squirrel?" HA! That's why our leader keeps asking us to A-R-T-I-C-U-L-A-T-E. Put the *d*'s and *t*'s on the ends of the words.

August 17, 2014

Two boys still struggling with their strep infection, and though the antibiotic has certainly kicked in, the awful cough remains, explaining my tired, achy, grouchy self this morning. Almost too much for this *elderly* lady.

Gene and boys got in the van to go to school when I see his garage-door opener lying on the counter. I grab it and run out through garage as he pulls out.

Unbeknownst to me, the puppy has squirted out the door and is doing eighty-five MPH laps around the yard and out into the circle. The boys spy her, they and Gene jump out of the van, and the four of us are chasing this seven-pound dog at 7:15 a.m., me in my pjs screaming her name, each of us taking a swipe at her as she passed. I know my neighbors think we're nuts. She finally shot past all of us and made a beeline through the open door, slept for an hour. Think I'll sign her up for the dog races.

Every now and then, Gene breaks out singing, "Way down in Columbus Stockade, wanna be back in Tennessee…go on and leave me if you want to, never let me cross your mind. In your heart, you love another, leave me darlin' I don't mind…" etc. I heard Tate singing it the other day. I'll bet he'll always remember his pawpaw singing that. As Tyler would say, "It'll be a family tradition."

"When I consider Your heavens, the work of your fingers. The moon and the stars, which You have ordained. What is man that You are mindful of him?" (Psalm 8:3–4). My eyes usually fly open about 5:00 a.m. I stumble to the kitchen, turn on the coffeepot, then let puppy out. Standing on the patio and gazing up at the stars suspended in space and absolutely brilliant this past week, I am so overwhelmed by this beautiful display of God's handiwork. I can only stand there and say "A‌L-LE-LU-IA, AL-LE-LU-IA, THE MAJESTY AND GLORY OF YOUR NAME."

Our puppy must have royalty in her DNA, thinks she is a princess or something. She will *not* eat her canned food unless I warm it in the microwave, then put a little on my finger and let her "taste-test" it. She's been taught by the best. Every man, dog, and hamster in this house is spoiled rotten, and I'm pretty sure I caused it. I will kick myself if I am ever able to lift my leg that high again.

Fuz, the hamster, passed away peacefully in his sleep on Thanksgiving Day. He is still lying in a box (not pine) but on a bed of pine shavings, in the garage (cold storage) awaiting a "service" if I ever get his little grave dug down in the corner of the back yard. I was his chief cook and bottle washer, cage housekeeper, giver of soothing emotional support and nightly cuddles. I'm sure I will survive. The boys took the loss like water off a duck's back. Oh well, our loss is "hamster heaven's" gain. Missed but not forgotten, Fuz bunny.

During a little getaway to Natural Bridge, Slade, Kentucky, this past weekend, Tyler asked, "Neena, when you were young, was *everything* black-and-white, or just TV?"

So Tyler gets off the bus wrestling an instrument case large enough for him to hide in. Two hours later, he stopped blowing. The baritone is lovely! I can see we are going to have a long winter. Of course, Tate gets his trombone next week. Actually, I love that they are interested in playing instruments. I've tried to "bend" them in that direction and then pray real hard that I don't lose the rest of my mind.

January 19, 2016

We were aware that one of the two fish (one for each grandson) would die during the night. I was planning a teaching moment about death etc. for the boys when they got here today, complete with a funeral, the fish in a little white box on a bed of cotton, burial in the corner of the yard. When I awoke this morning, my dear hubby says, "Hon, the fish died, and I flushed him down the toilet." Thanks a lot, dear.

February 29, 2016

At Great Clips, waiting for Tate to be called for a haircut, another grandmother is complaining to hairdresser about the little boy's cut (obviously trying to get a free cut). Not even looking up from the game on my phone, Tate says, "Hmmmmmm, somebody's getting a little sassy." I think he meant "testy."

April 19, 2016

It was a chilly day at Louisville Zoo but turned out to be a great day. Discussing what souvenirs they wanted:

TYLER. I want a green plant.
TATE. I want a girl monkey.

(What's up with that?)

October 1, 2016

Finally, a little brotherly love. Tyler carrying brother's trombone home from the bus. Just makes my heart feel warm and fuzzy. Gives me a glimmer of hope. Tyler chose to play "tuba" this year because they don't have to wag it home. (Tyler will do anything for his little brother.) "Love one another" (1 John 3:11).

July 9, 2017

I am not a fan of hermit crabs. When the boys moved, they left two for me to care for. Other than spiders and snakes, I have no heart for murdering anything that God created, but for the life of me, I keep wondering what these hairy-legged, beady-eyed creepies are good for. After months of prayer and supplication, "Batman" passed away peacefully. "Curious George" refuses to bite the dust. I'll think he's dead, put him in the bathtub, go back later, and he's crawling around, probably laughing 'cause he fooled me again. Little possum. So ready for him to join Fuz the hamster, Froggy the African dwarf frog, Hosea Rodrigues Gonzales the beta, and Batman the other hermit crab.

January 25, 2018

Our neighbors got their three-year-old German shepherd a "little brother" puppy for Christmas. Big brother is teaching little brother how to bark—at 4:00 a.m. every day, *right outside* my bedroom window (YAY!).

July 5, 2018

Feet hurting and ready to head home when I walked a nursing home resident back to his room after his haircut. He insisted on explaining each photograph on the wall which told the story of his life. Then he said, "But here's what I live by," and showed me a plaque on the wall that read, "Because He lives, I can face tomorrow." What a witness! We stood in his doorway singing that chorus as he beamed, and I heard an aide pass who began singing as well. My day was blessed!

Write down your favorite memories with your grandchildren on these journal pages

_____
_____
_____
_____
_____
_____
_____
_____
_____
_____
_____
_____
_____
_____
_____
_____
_____
_____
_____
_____
_____
_____
_____
_____
_____
_____
_____
_____
_____
_____

*Write down your favorite memories with your
grandchildren on these journal pages*

_____
_____
_____
_____
_____
_____
_____
_____
_____
_____
_____
_____
_____
_____
_____
_____
_____
_____
_____
_____
_____
_____
_____
_____
_____
_____
_____
_____
_____
_____
_____

4

Sin Is a Trap—("It's All About Me")

2008

Tyler's kindergarten teacher inquired about a place on the front of his ear. He quickly made up a story, "Me and Daddy went 'sploring at Veteran's Park, and a big black snake bit me." (Okay. Maybe he'll be a fiction writer one day.)

No Date Posted

TYLER. Where's my McDonald's bag?
TATE. WHERE'S MY MCDONALD'S BAG?

Erik. Aw shut up, neither one of ya has a McDonald's bag.

(This is what I could hear during my conversation with Erik.) They were in Erik's work truck, and each thought the other had a McDonald's bag.

January 3, 2012

The other day, after I used the word *crap* to describe a mess in the garage, six-year-old grandson exclaimed, "Ohhhhhh... Neena, Pawpaw's gonna wash your mouth out with soap." (Guess I'd better watch my mouth or buy some chocolate-flavored soap.)

May 30, 2012

Gene, Erik, and the boys have gone to the Legends game. What a day. First, we hooked up the Slip 'N Slide until they had soaked everything in sight, especially me. I climbed up on a chair to tie the four corners of a sheet to tree branches to create a canopy under the trees. The boys brought out their basket of markers and notebooks and made important signs like "Do Not Enter." We had chocolate and strawberry milkshakes. When T punched T in the back, I made him come inside and write ten times, "I will not hit T in the back." Looks like the notebook will be full by the end of summer. We made a golf course using some cups down in holes left from digging out sticker bushes, as well as the accordion thing that attaches to the downspout, four empty gallon ice-cream buckets, Erik's golf clubs, and a bucket of golf balls. As my great-niece used to say, "I peepy tired." And this is just the first of five days. Can't wait to see what we'll do tomorrow?

August 2012

Tonight it was my turn to say prayers. Lying between T and T in bed, I said, "God, please don't let me have a mean face when I fuss at the boys." Tate quickly piped up, "Neena, you don't look mean when you fuss at us. We deserve it." (Even the child realizes that discipline is important, and he actually desires it. Boundaries make them feel safe and loved.)

It all began innocently. Construction paper, toilet tissue rolls, Scotch tape. Before long, it escalated into a bean-spitting battle. This morning I am gathering pinto beans from my hall floor, and those are the ones I can see. The joys of boys!

Tate's teacher sent a note home Friday that Monday would be pj day in her class. So he chose a pair with footballs. On the way to school Monday from the back seat, Gene heard, "Pawpaw, today is not pajama day, it's tomorrow." After asking Tate several times, Gene pulled over, called me, and told me what Tate had said. I knew the note said it was Monday. So he said, "Tate, tell me the truth. Is today pajama day or is it tomorrow?" Finally Tate said, "It's today." He got to do thirty minutes in time-out after school for that little trick. It was kinda funny though, after the fact.

Lying on the bottom bunk with Tyler after they came home from their other grandmother's, they began to tell me that some of their cousins also spent the night at Meemaw's, and they told scary stories and generally terrorized my little Tate. Tyler started to tell a story, and Tate would cry, "YOU'RE SCARING ME." Tyler would say, "Okay, I won't scare you anymore." In a heartbeat, he'd repeat his previous action. There must have been something about Chihuahuas because Tyler mentioned that word, and Tate would became hysterical. Tyler said (with an evil smile), "Okay, I won't do it again." About a minute later, he said, "I'm just gonna sing a little song…about

Treasures from the Bunk Bed

CHIHUAHUAS," and Tate screamed again. Thought they'd never go to sleep. They both probably dreamed about Chihuahuas.

December 10, 2012

My life is anything BUT boring. Last night our doorbell rang, and our youngest grandson thought it was his dad. He peeped through the window, came into the kitchen, and said, "Neena, wonder why there's a cop at the front door?" Well, it appears he was playing with the phone a few minutes before that and dialed 911. Needless to say, he had his pj's on, teeth brushed, a lecture by the policeman, a stronger one by Pawpaw, and in bed within the next five minutes. Even the heart of an extremely intelligent child is full of foolishness.

January 23, 2013

One of the boys whacked the other in the back, so he retaliated by kicking the other one in the stomach. After the storm passed, one was praying and said, "I will NOT forgive him." I said, "Well, God says He can't forgive you until you forgive that person." He quickly said, "Okaaaay, God… I guess I forgive Tate."

February 11, 2013

Two brothers each with a strong will and need to be first and best is a recipe for many confrontations. Today's battle started over how many chapters there were in each boy's library book. Tyler's book won out with thirty-nine chapters. Tate's book had thirty-one chapters. And I know they are related to me because it had to be proven to both by looking at the Contents page.

March 24, 2013

Tyler's bedtime prayer went like this: "God, thank you for me, Tate, Mommy, Daddy, Neena, Pawpaw, Sheri, Otto, Pam, David, Uncle Gary."

Tate interrupted, "Tyler, your friend Jase called you a nerd."

Tyler said, "Neena, do I have to turn the other cheek if Jase punches me?"

I said, "Well, you should try to settle things before you get punched because your body belongs to God, and we don't want someone to hurt His property."

He continued his prayer, "Well, God, maybe you could just give Jase a wedgie, please? A really big one."

March 27, 2013

Last night, after wrestling the two wildcats to bed, Tyler wanted a drink. He is a little camel, but his brother is NOT. Tyler said, "I know Tate would like some water."

So of course, little brother decided, "Neena, I'm thirrrrsty. Can I please have a drink of water?"

"No, you can't, you know what happens."

So Tyler kept saying, "I know Tate is thirsty, aren't you, Tate? You want some water, don't ya? I bet a bottle of water would taste good right now, huh, Tate? Neena, get him a bottle of water. I bet your mouth is dry, isn't it?" He wore out the word *water*, and I guarantee you he did it on purpose. Wise little toot!

March 27, 2013

I could get on a soapbox about now. Too bad they don't seem to teach character traits (i.e., honesty, respect for the property of others). Of course, many aren't taught at home either since it's more popular these days to take from those who have something I want but didn't work or pay for. I'm going to make a trip to school this morning to rummage through piles of nasty, filthy lost-and-found items, knowing from experience that the jacket is not there. I suspect the same little second-grade vermin who took our cool Star Wars jacket in the fall has now "borrowed" our Southpole jacket. His teacher sent a letter home recently requesting no toys be brought to school because they are being stolen. AND we even see the Star Wars jacket on a kid, but stupid me, I didn't put our name in that one. Of course, we suggested that maybe a kid took it that needed a coat. Tate said, "Well, I've seen that same kid wearing five different coats lately." Observant!

Though I didn't pray for God's wisdom at the time in my struggle to find truth over who actually had the favorite quilt first (just before bed), I found myself suggesting, "Well, okay, since you both say you had the quilt first, I guess I will have to cut it in half and give half to each one of you. Now, where are my scissors?"

"No, Neena, please don't cut the quilt. Tate had it first."

Truth stepped forward. Then I remembered and related to them the story of the two women (they don't even know what prostitutes are, praise God) in 1 Kings 3:16–27 who each claimed the baby was hers. King Solomon told them he would have to divide the baby in half. The real mother cried, "No, give my baby to her, do not divide the baby in half." So the king knew who the real mother was.

(Thank you, Father, for putting words in my mouth. I pray the boys will remember that sometimes it takes drastic measures or threats to exact the truth.)

HELL HAS NO FURY like a grandmother whose grandson was bullied by three classmates, bending his arms back and kicking and bruising his legs. To make matters worse, the perps were three girls. I've already had conversation with the teacher who assured me "the girl" (one girl?) had consequences (yeah, I bet—pobably lost three minutes of her recess time). This is the same grandson who wants to give his friend money to buy books because he won't have any. And Tyler also told me, "Neena, I would never bully anybody. That's just the way I roll." It is a challenge to teach that though we live in a world full of evil, as Christians we must continue to be kind and loving and pray for our enemies. I didn't tell them that when I was growing up, we did not call them bullies; we had another more graphic name (and it did not contain a curse word). Today's teachers deserve *every* penny they are paid, and then some.

This week, Gene has trapped seven ground squirrels and transported them to the park. It was interesting to watch them as they were each seduced by a big red juicy strawberry, so completely irresistible. It looked delicious, it smelled wonderful, and boy, would it taste good. One little guy even managed to slip in the trap, grab a bite of the berry, and slip back out. We watched as he rounded the cage once again, and you could just read his little mind as he thought, *Hey, that was easy-peasy. I think I'll go in for the whole enchilada.* So he looked around, scooted in, took a bite and—*whack.* The doors slammed shut on his plans for a future at the Traugott's strawberry cafe. In telling the boys about it that evening before prayers, it was a good lesson for them: giving in to temptation can bring disastrous results. SIN IS A TRAP!

After church on Mother's Day, we all came back here to do steaks and burgers. We ate lunch, I washed pans, wiped interesting stuff from the counter and table, some A.1. sauce off the floor, tossed the dirty rag in the sink, then out to the patio. Erik bought the boys a treat from the ice-cream man. Tate picked a blue frozen dessert. We laughed about the big blue ring around Tate's mouth, blue teeth, and tongue. Erik said, "Tate, go in the house and wash your mouth."

He came back out in a few minutes, and I said, "Did you use a paper towel?"

He said, "Naw, I just used that rag lying in the sink."

Erik, shaking his head, said, "I KNEW IT... I just knew it..."

We had a great Father's Day. Tyler and Tate wanted to go to "big church" today, so I thought, *What the heck, it might be nice.* Well, I remembered to take paper, and they both made cards for their dad, then Tate wanted to go to the bathroom, then decided to check into children's church. Tyler stayed in church. He made airplanes out of the bulletins and one of his Sunday school cards. He actually managed to get a couple off under the pew in front of us before Gene caught him and made him stop (party pooper). Later, I looked over at him, and he was using one of the pens to draw things on his legs since he was wearing shorts. When he gave his card to his dad after church, Erik said, "Tyler, that's a great poem. Is that my picture there? What is that circle?"

Tyler said, "That's your belly." (Ha.)

When our munchkins were telling us about their fun at Coney Island last Wednesday, Tate told us his tennis shoes and socks were all wet because he "fell in" the lake. We found out today from his chaperone that he didn't fall in at all—he just hauled off and jumped right in. Big surprise! (That's why at that age, they have to have chaperones.)

Truthfulness (or lack thereof).

As I checked into a doctor's office today, the office is set up so that there are doctor offices located behind a door which is entered by each doctor using a card to unlock that door. I looked up just as the door closed right after Tate had tossed his flip-flop through the door. It was eventually retrieved after a doctor unlocked and came out through the door. All the patients waiting were having a good laugh. I never know what will happen next. Ah, the joys…

ME. Tyler, brush your teeth.

TYLER. I did it already.

ME. You did not brush long enough.

TYLER. But my toothbrush is wet. See? You're saying I'm a liar?

ME. I'll prove it, get me the flashlight. There, I still see Oreo cookie in your back tooth. Brush again.

TYLER. DON'T JUDGE ME! You're judging me.

As I lay in bed, I became impressed that there was a spiritual lesson in there. This morning as I supervised the brushing, I told Tyler how we can fool people on the outside (like the wet toothbrush), but we can't fool God who can still see the "Oreo crumb" (sin) on the inside, and God doesn't need a flashlight.

October 26, 2013

On the way to Louisville Zoo, I heard Tate ask, "Dad, do we have to have food and water to live?"

Erik said, "Well, you couldn't live very long without it."

Tyler piped in, "Yeah, Tate, that's why God made McDonald's."

November 5, 2013

Discussing (at bedtime, of course) the letter sent home yesterday about a fifth grader who brought a lighter to school and set several pieces of toilet tissue on fire. Some other students yelled at him, and he threw the paper in the toilet. Tyler remarked, "I bet that student got expended."

November 18, 2013

Every day is a new challenge. When Tyler got in the car after school, I would describe his demeanor as PUFFED UP! I could tell something had his dander up (as my mom used to say). So I asked him about it.

TYLER. Neena, a fifth grader called our Tate the A-word today.
ME. Just remember, when someone uses crude language, it just shows he doesn't have much of a vocabulary.
TYLER. And, Neena, that's not all…he called me an a-hole, and he said my whole family was all a bunch of a-holes.

(Momma also said sticks and stones may break my bones, but words will never hurt me. Well, that's debatable.)

January 7, 2014

Tyler especially liked a story about Abraham Lincoln defeating some bullies. He has had occasion to feel bullied. Tate, on the other hand, would just punch a bully and move on like he did recently when they spent the night with a neighbor boy. The kid suggested some pretty shocking stuff, and he called Tyler a dirty name. They told us all about it and decided themselves not to play with him anymore. They made their own "moral" decision. I was so proud of them and thankful to God they were both there. They told me, "We'll stay in today since we don't have any friends now." Tyler piped up and said, "Tate, yes, we do. We have each other." (Yes, we gotta stay on our toes, guys. Satan desires the heart and souls of our children.)

January 19, 2014

The boys were playing a game in the kitchen when Tate became angry that he had lost and shouted ——. I jumped up and ran in the kitchen, asking him what he just said and where he had ever heard such a thing. He repeated it and said, "Chase."
I said, "Don't you *ever* say that again."
He said, "Why?"
I said, "'Cause it breaks God's heart to hear us say things like that."

He looked at me and said, "But, Neena, I don't even know what it means."

Tyler said, "Oh, I know, it probably means s-e—you know." (They never do finish spelling s-e-x.)

Your best excuse will not cut it with a disappointed child.

After his shower tonight, Tyler lifted his arm and said, "Neena, I think I feel hair under my arm. See if you can feel it."

Knowing he was hopeful, I said, "I think you're right, sure feels like it."

Later, in bed, he said, "I think my voice is changing too? Tate, I have hair under my arms, don't I, Neena?"

Tate hesitated and said, "Well, I have hair on my chest, and I have hair on my legs too."

Tyler said, "So do I, Tate. Neena, turn on the light and see if I have hair on my chest."

I said, "Oh, wait till tomorrow, Tyler, and we'll look at your chest...with a magnifying glass." I told them that bodybuilders sometimes shave off all their body hair.

Tyler said, "I do *not* want to be bald all over, like a baby's butt."

I thought I'd never go to sleep. I laughed for at least thirty minutes after I got in bed. Guess hair or the lack thereof is important to the male gender, even at eight and ten.

Talking to Sheri on the phone while waiting for Tate to finish his shower. I had on my pjs and robe. I heard some ticking from my robe pocket, reached in there, and the thing went off. I yelled, "It's a grenade!" I thought Sheri was coming through the phone. Then when I told her, "It's a toy," we had a good laugh. They threw that thing down the hall and yelled, "TAKE COVER—GRENADE!" The grenade was left in my pocket because Tyler had been wearing my robe.

Yesterday afternoon, Tyler got out the tray of mini cinnamon rolls and sat them on the table. There were only four left, and I told him to take two and leave two for Tate. He quickly leaned over and licked the tops of all four rolls, looked up, and said, "He won't want any now."

TYLER. Why do we have to go to school anyway?
ME. Because it is a law in this country.
TYLER. Can't we just move to another country?

We were driving home from basketball practice, Tyler in the seat next to me, Tate in the back with Gene, discussing how all the boys were not acting very nice. Gene said, "Tate, I saw you talking back to the coach a couple of times."

Tate said, "Well, that other guy knocked me down, and it was his fault."

Tyler leaned closer to me, rolled his eyes, and softly said, "Yeah, that's what they all say."

March 1, 2014

Challenged all day by a strong-willed ten-year-old, I can be pretty strong-willed myself. The last line drawn in the sand was "go in the bathroom and take your shower."

He. No, I'm not going first.
Me. Oh yes, you are.
He. No, I'm not.
Me. Yeah, I think you are. So you gonna go the easy way or the hard way?

Guess who's in the shower at the moment. (It is *not* me.)

March 24, 2014

Sometime in the last five minutes of the U-K game yesterday, Tyler begged me to "turn off the game, Neena, your face is red, and you're scaring me." This is why I don't normally watch U-K basketball games.

March 25, 2014

One of our grandsons (not naming names) has an argument for *everything*. This morning went like this:

Treasures from the Bunk Bed

"Did you brush your teeth?"

"Yes."

"Come over here and let me check. You will never have a girl-friend if you have bad breath."

"Well, there are some girls who like bad breath."

"Sure there are, and when you bring her by, you can introduce her to me through the storm door. Go back and brush your teeth."

April 24, 2014

Once again, I was made aware that the meaning of certain words and phrases that I grew up with have a totally different meaning to this generation of children. Trying to get nine- and ten-year-old boys to get ready to go to Awana's, I told them to "lay down your tablets and put on your shoes so we can leave. You've been on those things since you got home from school. I'm tired of your faces being glued to all these boob-tubes around here." (*Wrong* wording.)

"NEENA, you just said a bad word."

"No, I didn't."

"Yes, you did, and we're gonna tell Brother Bill when we see him at church." (Guess I got busted.)

April 30, 2014

Last night, at bedtime, out of the blue, Tate said, "Neena, will there be marinara in heaven?"

It took a couple of seconds, and I said, "Oh, you mean marijuana?"

He said, "Oh yes, that's what I mean."

(We had been discussing this and other addictions recently. God's Word says anything that becomes a god in your life is a sin.)

June 6, 2014

(At the breakfast table this morning)
Stop making faces at me.

I'm not making faces at you.
Yes, you are.
No, I'm not. That's just my regular face.

Tyler was thanking God last night for all the people He has put in his life and began commenting on their talents. He said, "Neena sings and plays the piano and helps 'old' people. Daddy does good landscapes. Tate can sing and...well, everybody says...he's really cute." Tate had been listening, of course, and at that point, he yelled, "CUTE? I can do a hundred things and you just say 'Tate's CUTE?' I'm good at baseball, basketball, soccer, and all you can say is I'm CUTE? You really hurt my feelings, Tyler. AND you are wrong... I can NOT sing."

ME. If you don't get a better attitude, you are going to have a tough row to hoe.

TYLER AND TATE. Ohhhhhhh, Neena, you said a bad word. You said *ho*.

ME. Do you know what it means?

TYLER. It means a girl with two or three boyfriends.

(Okay? Yeah, that's partially correct.)

March 14, 2015

These kids just *have* to go back to school tomorrow. This is the longest week of my life, and it's just midday on Tuesday. Took Tyler to the "Y" yesterday, and he swam all of fifteen minutes. We just took down our "shooting gallery" on the kitchen counter. They have an arsenal of Nerf guns, and it was fun for a time. Now it's back to Xbox. That will last a little while, then a free-for-all will break out, then a period of separation. It's kind of a cycle. I forced Tyler to work on fractions yesterday, which made me REAL popular (teehee). Gonna be a loooooooooong day. I'm sure glad Gene is here.

May 4, 2015

Gene putting dishes in the dishwasher after dinner.

GENE. Who put his plate in the drain basket in the sink?

TYLER. I washed mine and put it there.

GENE. Well there's a spot that is not clean.

TYLER. Just one little spot? Well, nobody's perfect.

(Sweet Tyler, that one little spot makes the entire plate dirty, just like one "little" sin makes our whole heart dirty. Thank you, Jesus, for your forgiveness and the cleansing power of your precious blood so my "plate" [heart] can be spotless before you.)

I decided to try on a "skort" I bought a couple months ago. In front of the full-length mirror checking "things," I turned a little to the side and—oh well, I'll be…someone had sneaked in and inked a map of the whole state of Georgia on the back of my leg, just above my knee, in purple. My grandsons just can't get over these ugly spider veins. Maybe I'll just wrap an ACE bandage around my leg and wear this skort anyway. The boys made me promise not to wear shorts or a swimsuit.

July 7, 2015

Discussing our new schedule for evenings around here. I told them that at 8:00 p.m., all electronics, including the TV, would be turned off, and we will all read our Bibles for twenty minutes and something from the school library for twenty minutes. Then it's shower time, milk and cookies, and then all little monkeys are going to bed. Tyler says (with that mischievous twinkle in his eye), "Neena, I'll read my book from school for the book report and then read the maps in the back of my Bible. Will that count?"

Hmmm!

August 16, 2015

TYLER. I can't eat any more spaghetti. I'm full (7:00 p.m.).

ME. You have hardly eaten anything. I will save it, and when you come in the kitchen before bed and say you're hungry, I'll warm it up and you can eat it then.

TYLER. I'm hungry (9:00 p.m.).

ME. Okay, I'll heat the spaghetti for you, and then you may have something else if you want.

TYLER (to the dog). Coco, if you'll eat my spaghetti, I'll give you a BIGGGG treat, okay?

(It's all about me—bribery to cover your sin.)

Dear God, I just want to thank you for hearing my feeble prayers and answering in your time—time after time.

After karate class, the boys began taunting each other. We finally had to have a talk about the name-calling. Apparently, Tyler had been calling Tate "fat boy," and Tate retaliated by calling Tyler "Mr. Skinny Jeans." LOL!

I had been on Tyler's case for a number of reasons. I heard both boys discussing the fair.

TYLER. Dad's gonna give us some money for games.
TATE. Is Neena gonna give us some?
TYLER. You can ask her, but you better let her calm down first.

My shoe stuck to the kitchen floor over by the bread drawer. "Who spilled something on the floor, and what is it?" No one will take responsibility for anything anymore. They must have been watching the presidential debates.

Since I had promised him earlier in the week that we would go shopping for his Christmas gift to Tate, I was on the spot to take Tyler shopping when he came home from school. He knew exactly what he wanted to buy and he had twenty-five dollars just begging to be spent. We wound up at Dick's to buy the item, and he was ecstatic to wrap it straight away. Later, while saying our prayers, Tyler said, "I'm really worried now, Neena, 'cause I spent all my money on Tate, and now I can't buy presents for you and Pawpaw, Meemaw, Mom and Dad, and my cousins. What am I going to do?" I had already told him that you can't spend everything in one place; you have to budget your money or you wind up with bills to pay and nothing to pay them with. He said, "Yeah, I think I need to get a job."

"Welcome to the real world, Tyler-man." (Stubbornness must be in our DNA. I had to learn the hard way too.)

October 29, 2015

Well, Tyler's baritone mouthpiece is stuck, and we have all tried to get it off. It just won't budge. Had to hand-carry the instrument as well as the case. Concert is in fifty short minutes. I'll bet the band teacher will be really pleased about this.

December 5, 2015

Came home from a wonderful women's ministry brunch, getting ready to sit awhile when Tyler begged me to take him to do his gift shopping at the mall. There were "only" about five thousand other shoppers there. *Oh my gosh!* Then he had to eat at the food court. Then we had to stop at Walmart for more wrapping paper. Then he had to wrap everything TONIGHT! It is now 8:30 p.m. This child wears me out. Where is my Advil, bed, and heating pad?

October 2018

Tyler called me from school and said, "Some guy at school wants to fight me. What should I do, Neena?"

I said, "Well, I don't think God wants us to fight because our bodies belong to Him, so maybe if you could settle it before it gets physical, it would be better. But if that doesn't work and he hits you, take up for yourself. Just let him get in the first blow." Later he called me and said it was settled, and they are now friends.

When boys were here, around Thanksgiving 2019, Tyler said someone at school called him an "a-hole."

I asked "What did you do?"

Treasures from the Bunk Bed

He said, "Nothing. I just walked off."

I said, "Good boy. That makes you the bigger man."

He said, "No, Neena, he was way bigger than me."

We had to have a talk explaining what I meant by the "bigger man.'"

Tate called and said, "Neena, a boy at school came up behind me and hit me on the head. I said 'stop that,' but he hit me again. I busted him with my fist and broke a bone in my hand." Tate had to wear a cast for six weeks. Sometimes dealing with a bully can be costly (and painful). In Genesis, Noah was bullied and teased because he was building an ark like God asked him. He did it anyway, and God kept His promise to Noah and took care of him and his family (Genesis 6–7).

NOTE TO SELF: Take it from one who knows—DO NOT EVER LEAVE A BAG OF BROCCOLI CROWNS in the trunk of your car for eight (8) warm, moist days. We all thought something had crawled into my car and died, but we could not find it until one of the boys opened the little door in the back seat to peer into the trunk. ROTTEN ODOR? INDESCRIBABLE. I said, "Boys, that's how sin is. The longer you do it, the worse it smells."

*Write down your favorite memories with your
grandchildren on these journal pages*

_____
_____
_____
_____
_____
_____
_____
_____
_____
_____
_____
_____
_____
_____
_____
_____
_____
_____
_____
_____
_____
_____
_____
_____
_____
_____
_____
_____
_____
_____

Write down your favorite memories with your grandchildren on these journal pages

_____
_____
_____
_____
_____
_____
_____
_____
_____
_____
_____
_____
_____
_____
_____
_____
_____
_____
_____
_____
_____
_____
_____
_____
_____
_____
_____
_____
_____
_____
_____
_____

5

Prayer—God

*In that day you will say: "I will praise you, LORD, your
anger has turned away and you have comforted me.*
—Isaiah 12:1 NIV

Dear God, I just want to thank you for hearing my feeble prayers and
answering in your time—time after time. (Me)

"The best way for your child to learn how to pray is to hear
you pray with them and for them. Let your children hear you speak
words of adoration and worship, confess your sins, make specific
requests, and then thank the Lord again for listening and answering"
(Dr. James Dobson).

No Date

One Sunday, we were coming home from church. Tyler asked,
"Neena, where's God?"

I said "Well, God is everywhere, sweetie." In an instant, Tyler had the window rolled down, waving his hand in the air and at the top of his lungs yelling, "HI, GOD."

While praying, I am lying between T and T. Tyler's arm is across my middle, and I'm thinking, *That is so sweet.* Tate prays, "God, thank you for me, Tyler, Mommy, Daddy, Neena, Pawpaw—and, God, TYLER JUST PINCHED ME."

I love Tyler and Tate. Lord, be with them today. I pray for peace, Father. Peace for these two boys and myself. I love you, God, with all my heart. Bless my children and grandsons today really good.

Whew! Mornings are hectic getting seven- and eight-year-olds out of bed and ready for school, but the goodbye hugs and kisses are worth every minute of it. They were especially sweet this morning. I pray that their day is fun as well as productive. PRAYER:

> God, please protect their eyes from things they should not see, ears from things they should not hear, and keep their feet from places they should not go. Let them be children, free from all the evil in this world. Amen.

> PS: Erik was in complete control this morning while Gene and I got ready to go to nursing homes to sing with our senior choir from church, then to Golden Corral. Yay!

Tate was very tired and slept with me last night. I asked if he wanted to say his prayer. He said, "Neena, I like to hear you pray 'cause the words you say and your voice makes me go to sleep." Guess I could take that a couple of ways. For me, it brings peace and comfort in the chaos of life. Maybe even a child can sense that.

June 28, 2012

Our second grandson heard the soft knocking at his heart's door yesterday in Vacation Bible School, opened the door, and invited Jesus into his heart and life. We are thrilled. I had the feeling he would respond soon. I have lived and prayed for this day. Praise you, God, for this *amazing wonder* (prayer answered).

October 22, 2012

Gene was driving the boys to school this morning after a nice, calm start here. He always prays out loud for them (yes, eyes open). Halfway through the prayer, the fight started in the back seat. He said, "Okay, I'll just stop praying for you all if you're gonna fight all the way to school." Things became quiet for a minute, then Tate said, "Aww, Pawpaw…please pray for us. We really need it." We ALL need prayer—every day, especially two little guys facing a day in this ever-changing world.

November 29, 2012

Tate's prayer last night: "And, God, help Santa Claus to be safe when he travels all over the world and don't let anybody shoot him." We live in such a violent time our little ones have to worry about Santa getting shot?

Erik bought the boys each a bag of Dum Dums. After dumping all the suckers into a big bowl, I overheard Tyler say, "Look at all these suckers, Tate. God has *really* blessed us." A child's interpretation of blessing might be different from mine, but they're getting the picture.

March 10, 2013

I recorded the first of *The Bible* miniseries last week and played it last night for T and T. They were glued to the TV. I couldn't fast-forward through commercials fast enough, and I thought Tate was going to cry when it ended. They were excited to recognize the stories (like Noah and the ark and Moses parting the waters) that they have learned and read about. And *that*, friends, makes *my* boat float!

March 14, 2013

God will not protect me from something He can use to perfect me—Pastor, Wednesday night service (well, something like that). Wow! Maybe that explains why some of my prayers aren't answered *my* way. God must feel like I do when one of my grandsons stomps his foot and demands a milkshake ten minutes before dinner. There is such peace in trusting that God knows what is best for me. The older I get, the more obvious to me that I need a lotta perfectin'.

April 15, 2013

Nine-year-old Tyler came home today and, through moist eyes, told me that next week is bookfair, and he wants to give ten dollars of his own money to his friend whose father died last year so he can buy some books. He said, "Neena, he doesn't get an allowance and does not have any money." God love his heart. I love his heart also. I pray that he will always have that kind of heart.

April 23, 2013

Today was another bookfair day at school, and Tyler was excited this morning as he got out his allowance and put money in his backpack. He swore his brother to secrecy about the ten dollars he was giving to his friend. He said he didn't want anybody to know because it "might embarrass his friend." I wish we could all be like that, giving without having to tell the whole world about it.

April 23, 2013

Tate's bedtime prayer ended this way: "And, God, I'll give you my money. You are the only one I can trust with my money…but, God, yes, that's right—you don't need any money. So I guess I'll keep it, but if you need it, you can have some." "God wants you to not be greedy for money, eager to serve" (1 Peter 5:2).

Treasures from the Bunk Bed

June 20, 2013

Prayer time last night. Tate says, "God, thank you for everybody. You give us soooo much, and, God, we don't deserve it, but you do it anyway. Help me to get baptized. I really want to. And PS, help Scout [black Lab] and the puppy that died to have fun playing in heaven." (So sweet. Bless his heart!)

July 22, 2013

Although I am not doing what I imagined I would be doing at this stage of my life, I honestly cannot imagine doing anything else with my life.

August 9, 2013

Prayer time tonight. In the middle of Tyler's prayer: "—and, God, thank you for my life. I don't know what I'd do without it."

August 24, 2013

God blesses us through our kids sometimes. I found out that our son gave his lunch to a homeless man recently. I can't take credit for that but am proud for that kind of heart. Maybe it will pass down to the boys.

September 4, 2013

Sharing with Tyler last night that I had read that even when people lose their memories, they still have their artistic gift; i.e., music, painting, etc. His response, "I would give up my music gift so someone could get their memory back." (He's supposed to get his cello today for elementary orchestra. Can't wait for the Christmas concert. Ha!)

September 9, 2013

We and the boys had been so hopeful in anticipation of a certain family matter. It was to be yet another disappointment. Such is life, and we do have those things we have to face and move on. I always told the guys that sometimes God answers our prayers the way we want, but there are other times when God knows what is best and takes care in His time, and those are the times that make us stronger. Of course, being a grandmother, I truly believe that God uses us to bless our grandchildren as well. Well, in Tyler's prayer one night, through tears, he begged God for a miracle. It touched me so, and I will always believe that it was God who moved me to help with this particular "miracle," though God doesn't need any help with miracles. The next day, I asked God to show me how I could help with this miracle, and I was blessed that God worked it out through me. And that night in Tyler's prayer, I felt greatly rewarded when he said, "God, thank you for giving me my miracle." He was overjoyed, and I truly believe those times are great faith builders in the life of a child. How great is our God!

December 31, 2013

Partied with friends for years on New Year's Eve, but this is the best ever—Gene and I with our grandsons. Snacks on the coffee table, hot cocoa with cookies. Watching Fox channel, New York, waiting for the "ball drop" and doing the cha-cha in a big circle from family room through dining room and kitchen. This is what I call living the good life, and I thank God for this awesome privilege. Now, if I can just stay upright until midnight. HAPPY NEW YEAR, ya'll.

January 11, 2014

After last night's Upward practice and before the devotion, the leader asked if one of the boys would like to pray. Tate readily volunteered. He uttered the sweetest prayer, asking that God would "help us all to play really good, that no one gets hurt, and it doesn't matter if we win or lose, we'll still be winners." (This coming from a fiercely competitive eight-year-old was a miracle in itself.)

January 21, 2014

The two most favorite times of my day are early morning (5:00 a.m.) when I have my quiet time with the Lord and my coffee. The other best time of my day is when I lie down with my grandsons and listen to them offer up their prayers. Kids are so honest and say just what is in their heart. After they pray, I wait for them to ask me to say my prayers. It usually doesn't take long for them to go to sleep. I love to believe it is because it is somehow comforting to hear how much God loves them and asking God to prepare the little girls they will someday marry. I find opportunities to tell them stories from my own life as a little girl. Tate has shared with me that he likes to hear my voice when I pray. It must be a God thing. I just keep on praying until I hear deep breathing. I love it! What a blessing for me! "The Lord has heard my cry for mercy. The Lord accepts my prayer" (Psalm 6:9).

January 21, 2014

As a grandmother who wants to instill godly morality and Christian ideals in my grandchildren, I need a little help. How do you monitor what they watch on YouTube for example? I can't believe that we should just give them free rein on the internet and allow them to fill their minds and hearts with violence and garbage hour after hour. I want advice from others who have the same concern for their own children/grandchildren. And yes, I realize we live in a different world than I grew up in, but I still believe that there are some things that never change. We live in a culture that is robbing our children of their innocence. This is the cry of my heart these days.

During prayer time last night, I told them that when I was a child, it felt like we lived in a country full of Christians. Tyler said, "Well, what happened, Neena?" I told him that since our country opened its arms to anyone who wants to come here, many people came from all over the world, and lots of them don't believe in the same God we do, and so we don't have as many Christians here. He replied, "Well, that's a good thing, Neena, because when they come over here, we can tell them about Jesus." Mmmmmm, I learn much from the heart of a child.

It's bedtime, and Tyler is mad at Tate, so while praying he says, "—and, God, bless everyone but Tate." So when Tate prays, he says, "And, God, tell Tyler you did *not* hear that prayer." He continues to pray, then ends it, "Amen and amen." (Sounds like a preacher to me.)

My favorite prayer, resting, and info-gathering place is lying on the bottom bunk about eight thirty-five on a school night. Discussing why I love going to church:

ME. I get to learn more about God.
TYLER. Nobody knows *everything* about God—not even you, Neena.
ME. Why did you say that?
TYLER. 'Cause you know about everything.

(I suppose I'll let him think that for a while longer.)

I was already exhausted as we headed out to church this morning. After deciding we'd do Subway for lunch, they fought all the way to church over which one would share their footlong with me. Then I wound up with my choice of two six-inch subs. Maybe the Sunday school lesson was on sharing.

June 19, 2014

Our AC decided to just blow warm air for about thirty-six hours. We prayed at the dinner table about it. Well, obviously it registered with the boys, for at bedtime, there were questions about praying in general. It turned into a great opportunity to try to answer some questions about prayer (i.e., praying and giving God a time limit: "I want it *now*"), or praying for something and waiting for God to drop it from the heavens in our lap (win the lottery). If our prayer is not answered in our delivery time and method, we sorta get mad at God because of His answer. Oh wait, what'll really humble you is when you pray for something, and He gives it to someone else. God is constantly answering prayers that we haven't voiced because our intercessor knows exactly what we need and when. Sometimes His answer is an "interruption" in our lives that He will use to bless us. Guess I could say—been there, done that—got the T-shirt! ("Your Father knows what things you need before you ask Him" [Matthew 6:8:].) Sarah and Abraham were praying for a baby. God promised Abraham he would have a son. Sarah laughed when she heard she would have a son (Genesis 17:1–25).

July 1, 2014

Boys will be back tomorrow. Next on agenda: camp for a week with Porter kids. Our prayer is that God will so move in their hearts they will never be the same.

July 23, 2014

What did I ever do for laughs before these guys moved into my life? After rising early this morning, Tyler was looking at the fish tank (which also contains an African dwarf frog) and suddenly exclaimed, "Neena, Frog is dead. He's lying on his back, and his eyes are crossed."

July 24, 2014

I was telling Tyler about one of our family members who had lung cancer but did not know it until he had an x-ray after another driver ran a stop sign and hit him. Before I could take a breath, Tyler said, "God did that, Neena. He wanted him to know he had cancer so the doctors could get it out or give him medicine." *Wow*, God really blesses me through these boys sometimes. So good that they know God heals.

September 1, 2014

Riding home from church yesterday, Tyler said, "I learned something today at church. That some men asked Jesus why he was eating with sinners. They thought he should be eating with those who already believed in Him. But Jesus said, 'I am the doctor and I came to heal the sick'" (Matthew 9:12).

November 17, 2014

The boys finished their boxes for Operation Christmas Child today. I love seeing their joy in giving those boxes to children who will know the joy in receiving them. Win-win! There is joy in giving! "It is more blessed to give than to receive" (Acts 20:35).

December 17, 2014

TYLER. If God sends me to another country as a missionary and I get that ee-foo-bowl-ia, I'll just still stay there.

Treasures from the Bunk Bed

Every night I kneel at the side of their beds and listen to my grandsons' sweet prayers, then I pray God's blessings over them. They usually go right to sleep, but sometimes when walking from the room, I hear, "Neena, where are you going?" So I get back down on my knees and start praying again (that they'll hurry and go to sleep). Last night, I prayed for a solid fourteen minutes, stopping every little bit to see if their breathing had slowed down any. Hey, I prayed for friends, family, and neighbors, all the hungry kids in the world, great-aunts and uncles, first, second, and third cousins, all our past dogs and cats, Hosea the fish and Fuzz the hamster, and that grumpy cashier at Walmart. They were finally asleep, but to make sure my creaking bones would not awaken them, I rolled over on my hands and knees and backed out of their room with the dog under one arm. I didn't want to hear, "Neena, where are you going?"

Going to church this morning, I told the boys that if someone said "Happy Easter," they could reply, "Happy Resurrection Day." Coming home from church, Tyler said, "Neena, it's just like you said. Someone said 'Happy Easter,' and I said 'Happy Restoration Day.'" Well, at first I smiled. Then I started to correct him, but I thought, *You know, for the Christian, it is Restoration Day.* God restores my soul, and His mercies are new every day (Lamentations 3:23).

Bedtime prayers are where my favorite memories are made. Last night, a pop quiz:

> ME. I know that I'll go to heaven when I die because...
> I'm a good person.
> *Nope.*
> I was baptized when I was seven.
> *Nope.*
> I played the organ at church.
> *Nope.*
> I sang in the choir.
> *Nope.*
> I loved everybody.
> *Nope.*
> My daddy was a preacher.

Treasures from the Bunk Bed

Nope.

I was just getting started when Tyler said, "Okay, Neena, we get your point."

TATE. You go to heaven if you believe in your heart that Jesus is your Savior (John 3:16).

May 11, 2015

No time to arrange, but I had a very "floral" Mother's Day. Thank you, Gene, for the roses, Sheri and Otto for the dipladenia, and Erik for the hanging basket and plant. Tate forgot his creation at school Friday. He said it was for me. Tyler said, "Tate, she's not our mommy."

Tate replied, "Well, she does a lot of mommy things." God bless his little heart.

March 21, 2016

Tate is in the bathtub, Tyler sitting up on the back of the toilet playing a game on his phone. Erik is taking off a shirt to give me to throw in the washer. I walk by and take the shirt. Without looking up, Tyler says, "Hey, is this a family reunion or sumpthin'?"

April 29, 2016

Dear Lord, please keep these four busloads of band students, teachers, and chaperones in your tender care as they travel to Gatlinburg today. May their performance make their middle school proud. Assign a special angel to watch over our sweet Tyler. He's running on adrenaline this morning. Thank you, Father.

September 18, 2016

I love praying my grandsons to sleep.

Boys told me this morning they did not want to go to their grandmother this weekend. When they got home from school this afternoon, again they said they just wanted to stay here this weekend.

ME. Well, she wants you all to help her pack some stuff, and she'll pay you $20 each.
TYLER. Let's go. (Materialistic little mutts.)

Nothing can thrill like witnessing the absolute joy of a child whose long-standing prayer has been answered, and he can acknowledge that God answered the cry of his heart. That's a faith builder (and I am a hopeless romantic).

It seems just like yesterday that every night I knelt beside two little boys saying our bedtime prayers. Visiting me last weekend, one of the boys, in a much deeper fifteen-year-old voice now, said, "Neena, would you pray with me tonight" As we knelt beside the bed, I listened to his petitions, once again thankful that through one of the toughest times of my life, God has so graciously blessed me with a treasure that cannot be bought with silver or gold.

*Write down your favorite memories with your
grandchildren on these journal pages*

_____

_____
_____
_____
_____
_____
_____
_____
_____
_____
_____
_____
_____
_____
_____
_____
_____
_____
_____
_____
_____
_____
_____
_____
_____
_____
_____
_____
_____
_____

Write down your favorite memories with your grandchildren on these journal pages

_____
_____
_____
_____
_____
_____
_____
_____
_____
_____
_____
_____
_____
_____
_____
_____
_____
_____
_____
_____
_____
_____
_____
_____
_____
_____
_____
_____
_____
_____
_____

Funnybone

A happy heart does good like a medicine.
Medicine may add years to your life, but laughter adds life to your years.
—Proverbs 17:22

No Date Recorded

A few years ago, someone asked our daughter what she remembers most from her childhood. She replied, "I remember there was a lot of laughter in our home." That blesses my heart really good.

Fall of 2009

My son-in-love was a career firefighter for many years. While he was still fighting fires, he invited Gene and me to bring the boys by the firehouse so they could climb on firetrucks. They had a blast. I was taking pictures, and at some point, four-year-old Tate grabbed my camera. After chasing him around a couple of firetrucks, I reached to get the camera and said, "Gimme that camera, Tate, right now."

He pulled back and said, "Not yet, Neena, I want to take a picture of your mad face." (I wonder how many faces I have?)

January 1, 2010

Well, I'm on my way to give blood (if they'll have it) at my grandson's school because he wants a T-shirt and a pizza party. Boy, what we won't do for our grandchildren. Since being blessed with those two, I have come to understand God's awesome love for me just a teeny bit more. About the same time each night, I go back to the bathroom and take off the day's makeup and grime. This night was no different. I said, "Tate, I'm going back to take off my face." When I came back, he said, "Neena, how did you put on your night face so fast?" There's that face thing again.

January 30, 2010

I think one of my grandsons is going to be a joke writer. Sitting in the bathroom last night before his bath, he says, "Neena, does it stink in here, or is it just me?" (I'm still laughing!)

April 15, 2010

Going to church last evening, four-year-old Tate said, "Neena, you should ride a motorcycle."
I said, "I couldn't do that. I'm too old, fat, and ugly."
He said, "No, you're pretty and beautiful."
From the back seat, six-year-old Tyler said, "Yeah, you're hot and sexy."
Made *my* day, ya'll. God love 'em. (Beauty truly is in the eyes of the beholder, but I've warned them about making up those fibs.)

January 25, 2011

So with grandsons seven and five, pulling up to Subway Sunday for lunch after church to meet Erik and Gene, five-year-old says, "Wow, Pawpaw looks nice in his clothes."

July 13, 2011

It was a really good day to take thirty K-5 kids to Coney Island. Fun riding the roller coaster and bumper cars. Wish my chiropractor appointment was this Friday. Whew!

August 6, 2011

On a beautiful fall day, Tyler decided to sell some of his original paintings. He wanted to sell them for one dollar each. Here he is.

Tate came home from school yesterday with a loose front tooth. This morning, Erik says, "Mom, I'm getting my lunch ready etc. Can you pull that tooth?" Well, it's been a while, but the old piece of thread still works. One yank and out she popped. (Guess the tooth fairy will be making a stop tonight.)

July 14, 2012

Yes, the boys are back. Tate (seven years old) has developed a taste for our healthy vinegar-water drink (unfiltered organic apple cider vinegar with the mother). After pouring some, he wants it stronger. I say, "Yuk. Tate, that's too sour." He turns, looks at me, and says, "Hey, you have your opinions, I have mine."

Found a firefly (fake) in a Mason jar that lights up for Tyler. He loves it. I think he should name it *Horace*. Horacefly!

This morning, upon observing our resident ground squirrel, Gene says, "The little varmint is sitting straight up on his behind, and his paws are together as though he's praying."

I said, "Yes, he's praying that I didn't slap Vaseline on the new shepherd hook holding up that bird feeder." Well, he just found out his prayer wasn't answered as he jumped on that pole and slid to the bottom. I told the boys that he either needs firefighter training or enroll in pole dancing school.

After first baseball practice Saturday, I am riding in the back seat of the truck; Erik is driving, Tyler in Middle, Tate next to the window.

TYLER. Where are we going, Dad?.
DAD. Coach says you both need to wear a cup.
TATE. Why?
DAD. For protection.
TATE. Protect what?
DAD. Your "boy plumbing."
TYLER. Why?
DAD. When you get married, you'll need it to make babies.
TATE. How-a?
DAD. I'll tell you in a few years, son. (PRICELESS.)

Doing homework with Tyler. Checking one of his papers, I noticed his printed note to his teacher which reads, "I do not no if mom and clown and dad is 'post to be capital."

Okay, waiting in the car line to pick up seven-year-old Tate, passenger window down. Sun is nice and warm. I'm half asleep when a silver-blonde head (Tate) with sweat band, blue eyes, and glasses, wearing a backpack bigger than he is, stops beside my car, pops his head through the window, and says, "Heyyyyyy, wassup, pretty momma?"

I got my haircut last week. Well, I guess I got Daddy's "pencil eraser" hair because it pretty much stands straight up. Last night, I was commenting on my hair to Tyler, and I said, "See, you can smash it down, then it hops right back up." His answer was, "Let me try," and he began to smack me on the head (hair) in several places, yelling, "Wack-a-mole, wack-a-mole." (I must admit it was hilarious. These two guys have an answer for everything.)

Bringing the boys home from children's choir, we passed a police car who had someone pulled over. Tyler said, "What if someone ran from the police and climbed up in a tree? How would the cops get him?"

Tate said, "Well, they'd probably call out the SQUAT team. Neena, have you heard of the SQUAT team?" (Oh yeah, I think I have.)

November 13, 2012

It all began innocently. Construction paper, toilet tissue rolls, Scotch tape. Before long, it escalated into a bean-spitting battle. This morning I am gathering pinto beans from my hall floor, and those are the ones I can see. The joys of boys!

December 26, 2012

Yesterday after all the packages were opened and we were getting ready to eat, Erik asked Tyler, "Well, son, did you get everything that you were wanting?"

He smiled and said, "Yes, I got everything except that jet pack."

Erik said, "Well, I didn't get mine either, so I guess Santa ran outta jetpacks before he got to us." Heh!

February 5, 2013

Oops, playing in the snow with grandsons all weekend, I thought I felt a teeny scratch in my throat. Time to drink my raw, organic, unfiltered, with-the-mother apple cider vinegar drink. And for all you skeptics out there who gag every time I mention the vinegar drink, I have not had laryngitis *or* seen a doctor for anything for about four years. You should try it, find it in the "healthy" section of your grocery. Our seven-year-old grandson loves it. It is yummy! Try googling "raw, unfiltered, organic vinegar." You will find all kinds of information.

February 15, 2013

Looking for the right song for my alter ego, Lula Mae, I tried it out on grandsons. I finished and said, "Well, what do you think?"

Tate said "Shoooooooeee! That sounds awful."

I said, "Is it really, really, really bad?"

He said, "*Yes.*"

I said, "Great, that's just what I was looking for." Haha! Oh, the look I got was priceless.

Listening to a fantastic blues harmonica player on YouTube, I put headphones on Tyler and said, "Here, listen to this sixteen-year-old rock the house!"

Tyler looked at me and said, "What's happened to my grandma? I've never heard you say 'rock the house.'" (Never underestimate an old person.)

The best utterances from the boys always seem to happen just before falling to sleep. Last night, Tyler said, "Tate, money means nothing to me."

To which Tate replied, "Well, I guess you'll just live on the street...in a cardboard box."

Circumstances required me to take grandsons with me to the nursing home to hug on some folks yesterday. I asked the boys if they'd sing for them. Here's the song they did: "If I had a little square box to put my Jesus in, I'd take Him out and hug His neck and share Him with a friend. *But*...if I had a little square box to put the devil in, I'd take him out and *stomp his face* and put him back again." The two not confined to wheelchairs gave them a standing "O" and begged for them to sing it again.

TATE, *playing with his tablet.* Neena, what is this?

ME. It's an ad to sell you a membership to a dating service. Don't know why it's there.

     Treasures from the Bunk Bed

TATE. Why would I want a date? I'm only seven years old!

TYLER. Well, when those pop up on mine, I just go ahead and join 'em.

(Maybe that's why it was on there.)

May 27, 2013

Washing some blinds today. Every time I'd pull two out, Tate would jump in. Here we have it, folks, *Tate in a bucket*.

June 17, 2013

Eating leftover steak for dinner, Tyler took a bite of macaroni and cheese in his mouth, and then took a bite of steak in his hand dipped in A.1., which he licked all over before putting in his mouth. Gene commented on the cowlick right on the top of his crown, so Tyler just licked the A.1. hand and slicked that cowlick right down. (Gosh, I love these guys.)

Well, since the boys aren't here to say "Yuk, what is that smell?" I thought it would be a good time to make a pot of bean soup (enough to freeze). I'm having flashbacks of Mom's Monday wash day and the bean soup with pork jowl and onion smell permeating our little house. Tomorrow, I'll be cooking cabbage and potatoes. The boys *hate* that "aroma" more than the beans. Mmmm...good! (I hated that when I was a little one also.)

Sitting here wondering what it was I was going to say and I remember a little eight-year-old voice telling me a couple of weeks ago, "Neena, you don't have to say something about everything." So...guess that's all, folks. Have a great weekend.

At Holiday World yesterday, eight-year-old Tate is going into the men's room behind Tyler and in front of his dad, turns back around, and says, "Wow, Dad, some of those guys in there look like lumberjacks." BIG GUYS!

After eating some sliced cucumbers, Tyler began coughing and sputtering. I asked if he was okay. He said, "Yeah, it went down my breathing hole."

Treasures from the Bunk Bed

More fun times with kids from Porter. Yesterday on the bus going to (and from) Big South Fork Railway at Stearns, Kentucky. Gene and I were on the "boy" bus, and yeah, they were definitely boys. One kid to another: "Hey, I'll bet this fire extinguisher will wet your hair and puff it up." Another grabs a ball cap from one behind him and plops it on his head, which is way too small for that cap. "Hey, this thing is big. What are you, a bobblehead?" On the way back, they began trading the souvenirs they had bought like a gun that shoots rubber bands for a little glass bottle full of coal. Boys... I love 'em.

Last night as I lay beside Tyler during his prayer, he reached over and pinched my cheek, then in closing his prayer, he said, "—and God bless my Neena's fat cheeks."

My husband does not like to wait on anyone or anything. So true to character on Wednesday, he decided to get out the ladder to clean out the gutters in the front of the house. When I saw him, I said, "*No way* I'll go up the ladder and do it." So I got up there and pulled out nasty leaves and stinky water while he held the ladder so I'd feel more secure. We decided that I should run a blast of water from the hose down through the gutters, which of course sprayed dirty, stinky water back on both of us. We looked and smelled like we'd been cleaning out a septic tank, *but* we got 'er done. He came in later and told me some guy stopped by and said he saw us cleaning our gutters, and he'd like to know if we'd do his. I said, "Of course you said he can't afford us?" Oh, he's so funny!

August 21, 2013

Now that "Dad" has Xbox, the boys told me our place is "boring." Teehee.

August 31, 2013

Erik and the boys stopped over to pick up their bicycles on their way to ride the trails in Veterans Park, and I asked him to meet Sheri and me at the station to put air in my tires. Without even looking up, Tyler said, "Well, now that you all can vote, you ought to be able to put air in your own tires."

September 5, 2013

Tyler just asked, "Neena, could I have some chicken cut up in a bowl with soo-ey' sauce [soy sauce]?"

September 10, 2013

Went to Shriner's with Tate to get a second opinion. The doctor comes in after the exam and reads the X-rays, looks at Tate, and says, "Well, I'm giving you a clean bill of health."

Tate quickly replied, "Oh, I don't want a bill. Send it to her." (*Pointing at me.*)

That boy is quick, I tell you.

September 17, 2013

Driving home after picking up the boys from school, I told them their dad was going to pick up a pizza and bring it to my house. Then they were going to his new townhouse where he was going to straighten out his garage, and they could help. Tate looked at me, shook his head, and said, "I didn't make that mess, and I'm *not* going to clean it up." Hmmmmm, wonder where he's heard that?

Erik had given back the boys' numbered car-rider pickup hanger, so I laid it on the kitchen counter and forgot about it. Sitting in the car pickup lane the next day, I realized I forgot it and thought, *Oh well, I'll just write the number on a paper and hang it on the mirror.* The bell rang, there was a long delay, and there seemed to be a lot of confusion, kids wandering around, going to the wrong vehicle. I thought, *Oh gosh, there must be a security problem. Wonder what happened?* Well, here came the boys. They didn't have a clue but said something was wrong with the numbers. We finally pulled away. I got home, walked into the kitchen, and there lay the hanger. The number I had written down was their old number from last year. Lula Mae (my alter ego) does not have to look for "stories." Stuff just happens, ya know. That's life.

Took boys for eye exams yesterday. While in the chair, Tyler asked the doctor, "Can I get a pair of fuzzy glasses?"

She asked, "Fuzzy glasses?"

He said, "Yes, soft glasses that don't hurt my ears."

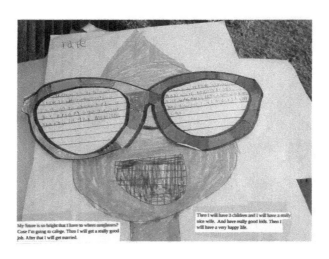

October 21, 2013

Sheri and Otto bought Tate a Bible cover for his new Bible. When he discovered it had a compass on it, he said, "That's great. That'll make it easier to find my Bible."

October 21, 2013

Logan's Roadhouse (after church):

TYLER: I want a steak.
ERIK: There's steak on the kid's menu.
TYLER: Where?
ERIK: Right there.
TYLER: That says steak *tips.*
ERIK: So?
TYLER: I don't want steak tips. I want a real steak. (Smart kid.)

October 25, 2013

Driving home from school, I asked T and T if they got enough to eat at the Chinese buffet with their dad last night. Tate said, "Oh yeah, and their crab rangoon was *really* good. It had more crab."

Tyler said, "And more *goon.*"

November 13, 2013

Lay down with boys at eight thirty last night. We heard phone ringing at eight forty-five. Tate said, "Why would anybody call at this time of the night?" Sounds like we're making little old men out of them. On a deeper level, kids definitely learn behaviors from the adults they are around.

Treasures from the Bunk Bed

TYLER. I'm gonna be a pastor when I grow up. I'll start with a small church, then a medium church, then a large church. Do you have to go to school to be a pastor? How do you start a church? I'll be the pastor and let Tate take care of the money and pay bills.

Oh yes, about an hour ago, I'm talking to my friend on the phone. Tyler comes and asks me to take off his outer pants over his tennis shoes. The conversation goes, "I talked to the nursing home today… Tyler, straighten your *foot* out…and we have the program… Tyler, your pants will *not* go over your shoes…on the eighth and twenty-ninth… Tyler, take *off the shoes*, you're gonna tear your pants… Oh, I've been praying for your mom… Tyler, just wait a minute, please…"

My friend says, "Linda, I'll let ya go, sounds like you got your hands full." Whew!

Kids never get enough, do they? My grandsons are out front using the snow Erik shoveled off the driveway to build a fort complete with a tunnel. I noticed a neighbor kid has on sweats that are soaking wet down the front and back; only the sides are dry. Boys!

Pulling in the parking space at our chiropractor, another couple about our age was coming out and getting in their car. We spoke, and the fellow said, "I don't know if you want to go in there or not. I think they're mad about something, and he's really jerking things around today." Haha.

Lying next to Tyler who was asleep in the first five minutes, listening to the sleet pinging against the windows, I was struck with fear as I heard gulping sounds from the upper bunk. I whispered, "Tate, are you going to be sick?"

He replied, "No, ma'am."

I said, "Well, what is that sound?"

He said, "I'm trying to see how many times in a row I can belch."

Tyler's project was "Majik sheets," inspired by his compassion and love for his cousin who was born blind. Tate's project was a toss game inspired by his quest for fun. Go figure!

Our ten-year-old grandson will eat almost anything, especially that twenty-five-dollar worth of cucumbers and tomatoes every week, and remains a string bean. The eight-year-old, on the other hand, who is very picky (though he will eat mac and cheese), is built like a candidate for fullback for the Dallas Cowboys. Tonight, I fixed some for him. He ate a bowl, then said, "Neena, this has to be the best mac and cheese you've ever made. It has a bunch of that saucy stuff in it." Now, that is a very high compliment, coming from one who turns his nose up at nearly everything I fix.

April 1, 2014

While the baby (puppy) sleeps, I'll do all my work. I cleaned out the refrigerator. I became hungry, but before I cooked my cream of wheat, I'd see if there was something in the garage fridge I might get rid of also. Well, when I opened the door, a can of cinnamon rolls fell out on the floor, the end flew off, and a couple rolls of dough squirted out. I salvaged what I could and well…had to bake them.

Guess what I had for breakfast? (As Flip Wilson used to say, maybe the devil made me do it.)

ME. What do you guys want for dinner?
TYLER. I want sketti.
TATE. It's not sketti, silly. It's *puh*-sketti.

Some people are just born to be nonconformists.

ME. Tate, what would you like for breakfast? Cereal, egg, toast, juice?
TATE. Just cereal, Neena.
ME. Tyler, what would you like for breakfast? Cereal, egg, toast, juice?
TYLER. I want General Tso's Chinese left over from last night.

Hmmmmmmmmm…okaaaay! Coming right up.

Commented to Tyler that when he goes, he can take the hamster with him. He walked to the hamster cage, looked Fuz straight in the eye, and said, "You'd better start packing your bags."

Cookies seem to last so much longer when the boys are gone.

Treasures from the Bunk Bed

Tate called from camp tonight and said, "Counselor and three of us boys are in the same room. We're gettin' to know each other *real* good!" (Haha, I bet!)

They're back. And incredibly tired. Should be an exciting afternoon and evening. I'm overjoyed at the prospects. Bet they didn't sleep eight hours the whole time at camp. I am glad they're home, but the rest of the day will be in the company of two sleepy grumpys.

This morning around seven thirty.

Me. Tate, what would you like for breakfast?
Tate. Bacon, scrambled eggs, toast with jelly, and chocolate milk.
Me. Tyler, what would you like for breakfast?
Tyler. Do you have any leftover pizza?
Me. Yes, I'll warm it up for you.
Tyler. *No*, I want it cold.

Tate pulled two threads out of his shorts today. Tyler said, "Tate, if you don't stop pulling threads, you'll be sitting there in your underwear."

Great fun at Kentucky Kingdom had by all. We rode everything except the twelve-story drop, although Tyler did the seven-story drop.

We stayed wet all day, and I'll be seeing my chiropractor tomorrow. Ouch!

July 31, 2014

ME. Do you guys know what a typewriter is?
TATE. It's probably something that you ride on.
He thought I said "type rider."
Apparently, I have never lost my Western Kentucky accent.

August 8, 2014

We shopped yesterday and the day before for new shoes and clothes for school. On the way home, Tate said, "I don't think I'd want to be really, really rich."

Tyler said, "Tate, I'm rich—in God's love." He must have been listening to the sermon, Sunday. He can be so sweet and, two minutes later, does something that makes you want to swat him. Gotta love 'em.

August 11, 2014

Walked through the family room this morning to pour my first cup of coffee, saw what appeared to be a sock in a ball on the floor by the front door. When I reached to pick it up, it moved. I jerked up as it waddled under a desk, then came waddling back out. I realized it was Fuz the hamster. I remember getting a phone call just as I sat his food dish in the cage. I apparently left the door wide open. Guess he had a fine night "out on the town." (Fuz probably found out that freedom ain't what it's cracked up to be.)

September 2, 2014

Going to pick up fresh-groomed doggie, Tate wraps the leash around his head and can't get it off. Thought I'd never get that knot out. Leave it to a nine-year-old boy.

Treasures from the Bunk Bed

Shopped for Halloween masks today. They got these, and they were so scared of them they would not sleep in the same room with them. I had to hide them in the guest closet.

So from the bathtub T asks, "Neena, when were we on fall break? Was it last week?"

I said, "Well, it was two weeks ago this Thursday. Or you could say it was eleven days ago this Thursday. Or you could say it was eleven days ago. *Or* you could say it was a week and four days back from last Thursday."

I heard him say, "You confuse me, woman!"

November 11, 2014

While decorating the tree (yeah, I know it's early), I dropped and broke three ornaments. Tyler fell on the sofa sobbing, "Those were my favorites." I explained that they can be replaced, but he didn't buy it. Even though I should've held them tighter, there are things in life which we need to hold loosely and let go, and others we need to hold tighter and never let go. His tears took me back to

Treasures from the Bunk Bed

Atlanta about forty-two years ago when his dad cried after Frosty the snowman melted. I think he eventually got over that traumatic event. Ha! (Note to self: be quick to catch future falling ornaments.)

Bedtime prayer. Tyler has made Tate a Christmas gift, and in order to let Tate know, he mentions in his prayer, "Please don't let Tate find his present."

Tate interrupts with, "You really should tell me where it is so that I won't have to look there."

Uh…

"Neena, where's *my* new toothbrush?" (From the bathroom last night.)

"What new toothbrush?" I ask.

"Tyler has a new toothbrush. Where's mine?"

"No, he doesn't have a new one. I haven't bought any new ones."

"Well, he just brushed his teeth with it. It's orange and white. His old one was blue."

Then I remember—earlier, I had laid my toothbrush on their sink because Gene had gone to bed early, and I didn't want to wake him.

Guess I'll be getting a new toothbrush.

Just sent Picasso Jr. off to school for Colonial Day. I think he should get an A for cuteness.

Shew, I'm sure glad the only things we brought to our house from the drum center were the drumsticks. Tyler is using his to play drums on my furniture, wood floor, our heads, and the last straw was when he got on the floor and started whacking the sticks close to my feet and yelling, "Dance, dance, dance!" Time to find a good hiding place for the drumsticks.

December 1, 2014

Taking boys to play their new drums:
Purse, check.
Keys, check.
Boys, check.
Drumsticks, check.
A good book, check.

Treasures from the Bunk Bed

Ear plugs—double check!

December 6, 2014

Discussing a school incident with Tyler, he said, "I would never bully anybody. That's just how I roll."

December 8, 2014

Watching *Columbo* last evening, Tyler, messing with his tablet, gets a mischievous look on his face and suddenly channels begin to change on TV, then turns off and back on. The little booger figured out how to program his tablet to do that so he can bug his brother. Leave it to these little computer-savvy kids.

December 10, 2014

Tyler always got excited when I had leftovers. "Can we have leftovers, Neena?"

Tate? Not so much.

Definite diversity in personalities and taste.

December 17, 2014

Christmas concert (middle school band):

TATE, *leaning over*. What song are they playing?
ME. I think it's "Mary Had a Little Lamb."
TATE. Doesn't sound like it. Every song sounds just the same.
ME. Well, next year you'll be playing those same songs.

January 30, 2015

Anyone lost a sock? I think I may have found it. Looked under my bed, and lo and behold, there were a dozen socks, some of which have been MIA for weeks. The little booger (Coco) was stashing them. Oh, by the way, there is also a partial pair of polka-dot underwear. Woohoo!

After a couple of attempts to get Tyler to go back and take a shower, we had to threaten, "If you don't do as I've asked, thus and so will happen," at which time he got up and went through the hall, doing the old man shuffle that Tim Conway did on *Carol Burnett Show*. He is definitely his father's son, the little stink.

Tate lost a tooth today eating a marshmallow. Between both boys, I almost have enough teeth in little plastic bags in my jewelry box to make myself a new set.

The boys have a friend over tonight. Sitting at the dinner table, Tate says, "My Neena can cut a cucumber really fast with a sharp knife and get close to her fingers but never cuts them." (Wonder why he chose that for a bragging point?)

Just before bed and prayers, Tyler discovered an ant on his foot and went ballistic (the kid who used to pick up every bug he found).
During Tate's prayer, he (devilish as he is) said, "And, God, make that ant that's still on Tyler's foot go away." And he laughed as Tyler freaked.

Cleaning up the garden so Erik can plant my tomatoes. Tyler lays his rake down with the tines pointing up (of course). Just as

I reached to turn it over and give a nice speech about safety, Tyler steps on it. The handle flies up and whacks me in the ear. Sporting a bruised appendage (lesson taught with nary a word).

The morning "funnies" really aren't very funny when someone else reads them to you.

TYLER. Would you buy me some springwater today, Neena?
ME. I'm going to buy what I always buy. I researched it, and it is fine. And it's cheaper.
TYLER. So are you a cheapscape?
ME. I think the word might be a *cheapskate*.
TYLER. No, it's cheapscape.

This kid will argue over anything.

Tyler's promotion from fifth grade to middle school is next week. He informed me I needed to buy him a tuxedo for the ceremony. Uh…well, I guess it's a big deal to him. (No tuxedo.)

After bath and weighing himself, Tyler looks in the mirror and says, "Neena, I think I've got a six-pack, or maybe a four-pack."
I said, "Well, I think that may just be your ribs, but if you work hard at it, you can probably develop a six-pack."

Boys love fireworks. The fourth was a very loud celebration. One of our neighbors must have shot off one thousand dollars in beautiful displays. Someone said that another neighbor has chickens. He and his family were out of town. We decided that he'll either have funny-shaped eggs or a bunch of constipated hens.

August 13, 2015

Tyler talked me into riding bicycles with him. Soooo trying to get on mine, my behind would not raise high enough to land on the seat, so the bike and I began to fall over to the right, with me grabbing the shelf in the garage next to me. Didn't quite make it, so after helping me up from the floor, Tyler asked in a worried voice, "Neena, are you okay?"

I said, "Yeah, just hurt my pride."

He answered, "Oh, I was afraid you were gonna die—but your bones must not be as old as you are."

September 13, 2015

Tyler is watching the Green Bay game. I'm singing an old hymn that is stuck in my brain for some reason.

TYLER. Neena, could you stop singing, please?
ME. God put this song in my heart, and I have to sing it.
TYLER. Well, could you just sing it in your head?

September 17, 2015

TYLER. Neena, I don't want to use those Stridex pads anymore. I want to keep my zits. They're a sign of puberty.

Tate decided to be a butcher for Colonial Days.

Brown beans and corn bread for dinner. Oldest grandson ate three bowls. Should get exciting around here tonight.

Came home from a wonderful women's ministry brunch. Getting ready to sit awhile when Tyler begged me to take him to do his gift shopping at the mall. There were "only" about five thousand other shoppers there. *Oh my gosh!* Then he had to eat at the food court. Then we had to stop at Walmart for more wrapping paper. Then he had to wrap everything *tonight*! It is now 8:30 p.m. This child wears me out. Where is my Advil, bed, and heating pad?

December 18, 2015

Tyler had trouble going to sleep last night. Finally, he said, "Neena, I don't count sheep. I count birds." I heard, "One"—fluttering sound—"two"—fluttering sound. He is a true nonconformist.

January 21, 2016

Another no-school day. Does anyone know of a school open within one hundred-mile radius of Lexington?

January 23, 2016

Sitting at the breakfast table this morning before the boys woke up. Gene was having eggs and toast while I was eating a half grapefruit. After a few minutes, Gene looked over at me and said, "What are you *doing*?"

"Well, that grapefruit was so good I had turned it inside out and was eating the pulp from the inside."

He said, "Oh, okay. For a minute I thought I was sitting across the table from a duck!" Guess the boys are rubbing off on me.

February 13, 2016

Sitting next to one of the boys, I said, "Honey, I'm going to try these new earplugs, so if you say anything to me, I won't be able to hear you." A minute later, I looked over at him, and his mouth was moving. I said, "I can't hear you at all, and I don't want to dig this stuff outta my ears. Send me a text."

March 15, 2016

Sitting in school pickup lane. Ten-minute power nap. Yay! Sure helps when the "whirlwind" hits.

Einstein is on his way to school. I just love being told that he had to dress in character twenty minutes before leaving for school. Had to cut a mustache from Elvis's sideburns (wig from an old Elvis show), root out a bow tie, Gene's old sweater, and grab a pipe from an old pipe stand. *We did it!* I just love a challenge at six-stinking-forty in the morning!

You know you need a haircut when your grandson says, "You look like Donald Trump."

May 11, 2016

Every morning at 5:00 a.m., I stumble to the coffeepot and take my first cup to the living room, where I have my morning prayer. This morning, as I lifted the cup to drink, there was something stuck to the bottom of my cup—a piece of paper that said "Weird-O."

August 1, 2016

We had the best day yesterday with our family at Kentucky Kingdom. While we were in the water park, I overheard one of our sweet little six-year-old girls making an observation: "Some people don't have anything under their arms, but some people have little puffs."

August 5, 2016

Found the perfect box for my CDs. I tossed the 4×5 air-filled packs on the floor. I arranged my CDs in the box, stepped back on an air pack, and I thought a gun had gone off. I haven't jumped that high since I was twelve.

November 16, 2016

One of my grandsons keeps his thoughts to himself while the other blurts it right out there whether you ask for it or not. I was driving him to youth group at church last Wednesday when, out of the blue, he said, "Neena, this van smells like old people. Your house smells like old people too." I suddenly remembered having the same thought when I was that age, and Daddy would take Johnnie and me with him to visit the elderly. Guess I'll be shopping for candles and spray tomorrow.

March 6, 2018

I decided to put on my makeup before my shower because boys were still asleep. While in there, I thought, *Aw, heck, I might as well go ahead and wash my hair.* So I washed it, towel-dried my face and hair, stepped out, looked in the mirror, and a "nekkid" raccoon nearly scared me to death. Had to redo the makeup from ground zero but still made my appointment. My life is so wild that I confuse myself.

April 14, 2018

TATE. Neena, what time is it?
ME. Well, that clock on the wall says it's nine fifty-one.
TATE. Neena, I can't read roman numbers.

July 15, 2018

Trying to clean out some papers and found one that is obviously from one of the youth weekends. Tate writes, "Purpose = determine what God wants you to do and chase it for the rest of your life—until you're retired." That's life.

November 4, 2018

A kid sitting behind us got the hiccups right after the Lord's Supper (communion) today.

June 21, 2020

Getting ready to eat Father's Day dinner yesterday:

ERIK, *asking sixteen-year-old.* Son, would you like to ask God to bless our food today?
TYLER. Dear God, thank you for my dad, thank you for letting me get a job, and thank you for this food. Amen.
ERIK. Tyler, that was short and sweet, buddy.
TYLER. Well, Dad, I'm not a professional pray-er.

Treasures from the Bunk Bed

*Write down your favorite memories with your
grandchildren on these journal pages*

*Write down your favorite memories with your
grandchildren on these journal pages*

_____
_____
_____
_____
_____
_____
_____
_____
_____
_____
_____
_____
_____
_____
_____
_____
_____
_____
_____
_____
_____
_____
_____
_____
_____
_____
_____
_____
_____
_____
_____

Reminiscing

These are a couple of stories that I can actually remember from my own children as they were growing up.

After my husband was deployed to Turkey, I bought a tape recorder, and we would record and send tapes back and forth. Our daughter, Sheri, would lie on the bed and talk with her dad. I overheard her say, "Can you find me now, Daddy? Can you see me?" Usually, I didn't know what she was saying until he returned from Turkey, and I listened through the tapes. One night she told him, "Daddy, I have some really *cute* things to tell you—and they're *all* about me." Being a daddy's girl made the separation very difficult for her, as well as for me. I have a great love for military families. They give up much for their country.

When we lived in Atlanta, Erik, our son, was about two years old. One day, I was highlighting my hair when I felt some panic that Erik was being unusually quiet. When I finished putting aluminum foil and a towel around my head, I found him sitting on the closet floor holding an almost empty bottle of Flintstones children's vitamins. He had eaten quite a few. I called his pediatrician, who told me to go to the drugstore and buy syrup of ipecac, so with my head wrapped in foil, I dragged Erik, and we made the trip to the drugstore. Since there was a food counter and it was noon, there were lots of construction workers eating lunch who stared at me, wondering where I had parked my spaceship. I got the ipecac and gave Erik a big dose before I left the store, asking every few minutes, "Erik, do you feel sick yet?" His reply all the way home was no. After following me upstairs, he said, "Mommy, I'm sick," headed for the toilet, and there went all the Flintstones. Erik, I, and my hair all recovered, but it has remained an unforgettable memory.

Treasures from the Bunk Bed

My memory just took me back to a holiday that I did not have to work. I was planning a shopping day. Just as I was headed out the door, the school called and informed me that my son, Erik, was in the office, sick. I picked him up, and by the time we reached the car, he was not sick anymore. When I asked, "You sure don't act sick. Why did you have them call me?" He replied, "Every kid needs a day with his mom, doesn't he?" Grrr, in hindsight, I should have marched him right back in the school. ("The Lord hates a lying tongue" [Proverbs 6:17].)

Then another memorable moment was the day that Sheri and my niece were babysitting Erik. They decided he should be dressed up in one of Sheri's old tutus (pink) and paraded him around the neighborhood. When they returned to our house, Erik got a little revenge by taking a bite out of Sheri's hand. When she ran and told her dad to get Erik in trouble, her dad said, "That's what ya get." Erik has never forgiven them. About the same time, my sister was sitting for me. The three of them walked to the pool, and on the way back, a construction worker whistled. Erik turned to the girls and so seriously said, "Did you hear those guys whistle at me?" LOL.

While my husband was stationed overseas and Sheri was four years old, a dear friend came to visit for Sheri's birthday. After opening her gifts, she became very quiet. I said, "Sheri, is something wrong?" She thought a minute and finally said, "It just doesn't look like my birthday." She obviously didn't care for the gifts. Though I don't remember the gifts, I do remember her obvious disappointment that she couldn't play with them.

Update as of Publication

Tyler is now almost eighteen. He loves playing tuba in his high school marching band. He has been working his first job in the restaurant business. He says his present goal is to be a band teacher.

Tate is sixteen and in junior ROTC. His Pawpaw may have inspired him to be in the military since he spent twenty-three years in the military. He is also working his first paying job in the restaurant business.

They are both talking about and looking at cars online. Typical boys. One likes Mustangs, the other likes Camaros. (Personally, I'm praying they both get little farm trucks.)

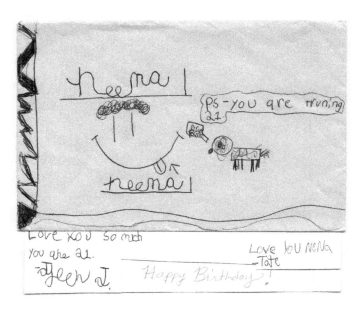

neena

ps-you are truning 21

neena

Love xou so much
you are 21.
-Teen J.

Happy Birthday!

Love You NeNa
-Tate

TATE

Daily Behavior Report

Name __Tate__   Date __9-6__

WHERE	CONSEQUENCE
● CLASSROOM	● YELLOW – 5 Laps
● HALLWAY	● ORANGE – 10 Laps
● CAFETERIA	● RED – 15 Laps, Call Home
● PLAYGROUND	● BLACK – Office

WHAT	COMMENT: got on the floor in
● OFF TASK	hallway and was walking
● HANDS TO SELF	like a crab
● TALKING	
● RESPECT	
● NO HOMEWORK	SIGNATURE:
● Not Following Directions	

SAnTA, CAni HAve
A PiCTVRe
foyOU PleS

145   *Treasures from the Bunk Bed*

AGREEMENT

I, Tate Traugott, agree to do my best to have a good time today and will
listen to Bro. Wayne and Neena when they speak to me. I know it is for my
safety and the safety and good time for the other people on the trip. I also
agree that if I have to be called down more than one time for not listening
which is being disrespectful, I will not be allowed to go on the next day trip
to Coney Island Amusement Park in Cincinnati, and it would be awful to
miss that trip.

TATE
TATE
June 8, 2011

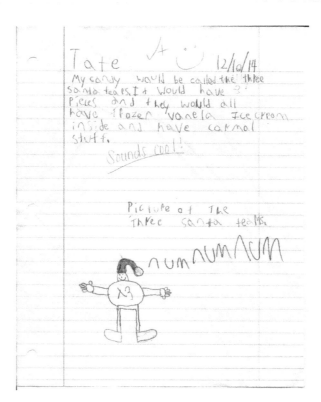

Tate   12/10/14

My candy would be called the three
santa tears, It would have 3
pieces and they would all
have frozen vanela ice cream
inside and have carmol
stuff.

Sounds cool!

Picture of the
three santa tears.

It I had a million dollers
I wold buy gifts for my pets
,dad/mom and grandparens. For
my pets I wold buy new toys.
I wold buy my dad a cherch shert.
I wold get my mom ten pars of shose.
I wold get my granparens two
chairs.

Tate was on orange because...
I was talking a lot and piano
making noise
    — making fart noises.

              4-16-13

what I want for 11-7-13
Tate Chrismes.

1. Dirt Bike
2. Nerf masher Gun
3. iPad
4. 5 amo packs
5. crazy lamp
6. A pupy dog
7. Basketball 2K12 for XBOX
8. WWE 2K12 for XBOX
9. stuft animals
10. A kitin
11. A Race car bed

12. Minecraft Lego's
13. Batman Lego's
14. Ningogo lego's
15. XBOX live mimber ship
16. Nerf sniper
17. Call of Duty Ghost XBOX
18. Tony haik for XBOX.
19. fireworks
20. momy
21. iFone
22.

Treasures from the Bunk Bed

How to build a good house

1. get 9 stacks of wooden planks. 3 stacks of cobble stone.
2. start to build the base of your house.
3. build it however you want but make sure it looks good.
4. start decarateing all of your house
5. do the finishing touches and make sure you like it.

TATe

If I Foud a per of Magic shoes I wod asc them to take me to Hawie and well have fun. and then I well asc then to go to dngsyland tell fast. After tha I well go into a vedeo game.

! How cool!

number 1

Tate ✓+ ☺ 12/9/14

I would wakeup then go in
my living room with monapaly.
me my brother and my grandma
would play monapaly. and at
the end I beatley won.
Then we went back to
my room and got Jenga
and we played that for
a while.When the game
was over I lost and my
brother won.Then we played
with our toys.Then went to
bed.

Very good job!

Treasures from the Bunk Bed

some kids bult a snow man and when they whent to sleep that winter night it came to life. So the next day they heard the snow man talking. It was Rambo colers so they put a hat on it and some butons on it. So the snow man followed them every woer all the time. One time they went by a fire and he started to melt so the kids added some more snow to him. One day he wonderd off and melted to the grond. So the kids looked for him and fond him melted on the grond so they bult him agen. So he learnd his lessan.

                                                    Tyler

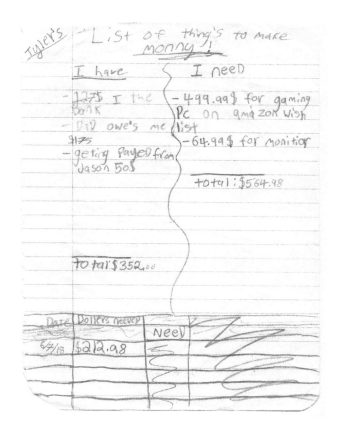

Tyler's "List of thing's to make monny"

I have	I need
- 127$ I the Bank	- 499.99$ for gaming PC on amazon wish list
- Did owe's me $175	- 64.99$ for monitior
- geting payed from Jason 50$	
	total: $564.98
total $352.00	

Date	Dollers neeved	Need
6/4/18	$212.98	

Treasures from the Bunk Bed

name: Tyler
teacher: Ms.willson

My Dogs tail

One aight I was a' sleep. I hed
my dog barking so I went to go
cheecki. My dog tail was cut in
hafe. So I went inside and told
my memaw that some one cut
the Dogs tail in hafe.

So we woke up my little brother
and took the dog to the animal
hospitql. So she go stiches and we
toolea the plole some one came
to ane house and cut are dog's tail
in hafe. They didn't find the people
but The dog's tail held.

One after noon the dog had a half
atack but she was a good dog. I Wish
we found the people but we didn't.
So we toola lile neaboors to wachout.
I didn't happen to no one eals.

Dear veteran,
thank you for your survece.
HOW was it Like in the air force
was it scary bad was it hard DID
you miss your famely did you rite
your famaly leters did you get shot
at did enething blow up did you
get to drive a tanek did you
drive plans so what did you drive
where did you slep what did you
what long ea into a teacher
what was in the army how many
pepole wer there. Thanck you
what you done.
            Love
                Tyle

TO: NeeN P&P&
FReM: Tylet

2013

by
Tyler #22

A group of people
were chasing a ginger bread
man and a fox ate it. This
is what he looks like. So tell
us if you find him. He is
real dangerous. Lock your
doors and don't go outside. He
will kill you. Tell us if you find
him please. He is a murderer on
the loose. He tricked the ginger
bread man by saying he could
not hear him. Then he grabed
him and ate him. So
be on the look out for
him. Keep your family inside
your house so they can be
safe. He hates everyone.
Don't trust him or belive
him.

The fox wander around looking
for people to eat. So watch
out for him because he
tricked the ginger bread and
ate him.

About the Author

Linda Tracy Traugott, who resides in Kentucky, is mom to two children and Neena to two grandsons. Growing up in a pastor's family, it was natural that she become involved for many years in various church music ministries as well as nursing home and prison ministries. She presently serves her local church body as accompanist.

Isaiah 40:31 'But those who wait upon the Lord shall renew their strength; They shall mount up with wings like eagles. They shall run and not be weary and they shall walk and not faint.'